Week-end Pilot

Frank Kingston Smith

Week-end Pilot

Vintage Books

A Division of Random House—New York

VINTAGE BOOKS EDITION, September 1974

Copyright © 1957 by Frank K. Smith

Library of Congress Cataloging in Publication Data
Smith, Frank Kingston.
    Week-end pilot.
    1. Private flying.   2. Airplanes—Piloting.
I. Title.
[TL721.4.S56 1974]   629.132'524'0422   74-5195
ISBN 0-394-71069-X

Manufactured in the United States of America

To my wife,
Marianne,
who has encouraged me to
rise above a sea of troubles

Preface to the Vintage Edition

For ages, people have wanted to fly and have wondered what it would be like to have the freedom of the birds, to wheel and soar far above the surface of the earth. But, at the same time, those very people have been deterred from flying, although the means of breaking the surly bonds of earth are available. Why? Because they are afraid. They are afraid of the dangers of flying and afraid of the costs of flying, and most of all, afraid that it requires some special talents possessed only by a few chosen ones.

Nothing could be farther from the truth. Flying need not be too expensive for the average person, and it certainly is not reserved for some special supermen or superwomen. As for the danger, I can report now from the vantage point of long experience that it is not as dangerous as most people think: Since 1955 I have accumulated 4500 hours; I lived on an airport for three and a half years; my three sons are pilots (one is an engineer at Piper); all of our friends fly; in the last decade my wife, Marianne, and I have flown to every one of the forty-eight conterminous States, all of the Canadian Provinces, all of the Mexican States and all of the Bahama Islands, right on down to the Turks and Caicos Islands—and I have never seen anyone hurt in an airplane, except at an air show or air race.

This story of my becoming a Weekend Pilot tells how I got started—and how anyone can get started—in flying my own airplane.

Try it—you'll like it!

Happy landings.

January 1974

FKS

Contents

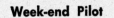

Week-end Pilot

1. So I Bought This Airplane

I used to be a positive type of person. Dogmatic.

I had firm opinions on all sorts of things—flying, for instance. Two years ago I thought that flying was strictly for the birds. This cavorting around in the ozone was all right for other people, but if I were going to kill myself, I would rather take gas. To my mind, flying compared unfavorably with mountain climbing, going over Niagara Falls in a barrel or standing up to my mother-in-law. I hate to think of violent endings, especially my own.

I have changed—to some extent, at least—for I now own and fly my own airplane anywhere, any time. But this was not a planned campaign; it came about purely as a quirk of fate. In fact, if anyone ever backed into flying, I did.

A few years ago, after a late start in the law profession due to the war, I thought I was settled down at last. As an attorney, father of three sons and co-owner with the bank of a home on Philadelphia's Main Line, I felt that I was becoming established both as a prominent member of the community and in my profession. I worked day and night, joined all sorts of organizations and clubs, kept several bartenders in silk shirts and bought a new car every year, to prove to everyone how successful I was. I lived by the motto "All work and no play makes jack." But, as many men before me have learned, there is more than a pecuniary price on success; I couldn't sleep at night, my stomach was always on fire and I couldn't relax—ever. My teen-age son referred to the old homestead as "Hypertension Hacienda." I sure wasn't getting much fun out of life.

Then one night, while attending a banquet, I went right over on my face in a dead faint. When I opened my eyes with the classic gambit, "Where am I?" there were three doctors standing around staring down at me.

"Nervous collapse," they told me with grave expressions.

I was thirty-five years old. I chafed at the bit while I was kept in bed, but the enforced rest gave me a chance to take inventory. "Slow down," the signs said. "Relax." "Take it Easy." I tried to make light of the situation, but life isn't particularly hilarious when you are flat on your back. When we are young and healthy, we take too much for granted.

So when I recovered and got back on the treadmill, I tried to relax with a hobby, or a series of hobbies.

Golf was my first mistake. At the Club I was called the "Civil War Golfer." You know, "Out in '61, back in 65." I got plenty of exercise chasing the ball through the rough and digging my way out of sand traps, but invariably finished a round more overwrought than I had started it. For me, trying to relieve tension by playing golf was like trying to put out a fire by throwing gasoline on it.

Gardening left me cold. Results are too slow, and it's

so seasonal. I must have some aptitude for it, though: I have some weeds in my yard that *nobody* can kill. My dog ruined the pachysandra, but the weeds flourished.

Photography was nice for a while, but my hands couldn't take the chemicals, and my wife wouldn't take my hands. So that was out.

Model railroading looked pretty good until my two smallest boys began to use the rolling stock on each other as weapons. Can you imagine asking a six-year-old where he got the bumps on his head and getting an answer like "I was hit by a locomotive"? Great for blood pressure!

The previous fall my law partner, Tom, had begun to take flying lessons, and each Monday morning he recounted his aerial exploits in detail. Having survived one war, three automobile smashups and fifteen years of married life, I was something less than wildly enthusiastic about Tom's tales. In fact, my reaction to them was like that of a bachelor listening to a yesterday-my-kid-said type of story from a doting parent—thinly veiled boredom.

On a Tuesday late in May, while in the throes of the mental depression that obsesses me when I am overtired and vexed with problems, I picked up an old copy of *Flying* in our waiting room and absently leafed through it. To my surprise, the people pictured in the pages of that magazine were not begoggled, helmeted daredevils, with leather jackets and high-laced boots. They were ordinary people, dressed in ordinary clothes: salesmen, students, businessmen, farmers, doctors—all of them with different backgrounds in education, experience and earning capacity, yet all of them had one thing in common: the love of flying.

I sat down in a comfortable leather chair and began to read with interest an article written by a young Roman Catholic priest, telling how he got his airplane. I knew that priests do not have much of an income, and I was curious to find out how he could afford it. It turned out he had bought a used Cessna 140 for less than $2,000, and that struck home, because that was exactly how much I had in the bank.

There was an almost imperceptible creak inside my skull, and just at that psychological moment, my partner walked through the waiting room with his arms full of law books.

"Tom," I said, trying to sound casual, "can your instructor find a Cessna 140 for me for less than two thousand dollars?"

His startled expression clearly reflected his reaction to my question—"Frank has finally flipped"—for he knew of my intense aversion for flying and my often-expressed conviction that it was too hazardous for a family man. He didn't know that I had just read the old edition of *Flying* and had concluded that if a priest, a grandmother or a high-school student could fly, I could too.

"I'll ask," he said slowly, squinting at me in a funny way.

Then the phone rang and we dropped the subject.

The following Tuesday morning, Tom burst into my office as I was opening the mail. His hat was on the back of his head, brim turned up. He looked as if he were about to burst.

"Bob Angeli, my instructor, knows where there is a 140 for sale in good condition and he wants to pick us up at Wings Field this afternoon so you can take a look at it and we can use my car to get there—O. K.?" he said, all in one breath.

I felt a quick tension shoot through my system that I hadn't felt since Navy days, when the red alert was sounded.

"O. K.," I answered offhandedly, wondering momentarily what I might be letting myself in for, and Tom rushed out of the office to call Bob.

After all, I hadn't really given the matter much serious consideration, and besides, my wife had her eye on (a) a new car and (b) a mink stole, in reverse order.

The whole day had a certain dreamlike quality about it; the next thing I remember was that about three-thirty Tom hurried me from my piled-up desk to his car and by four o'clock we were standing in the wire-fenced spectators' enclosure out front of the two-story operation office at Wings Field, surrounded by airplanes.

Wings Field is in beautiful rolling farm country about four miles west of the Philadelphia city limits, not far from Valley Forge. On it are based almost a hundred airplanes of all types: Beechcraft, Pipers, Cessnas, Swifts; twin-engine and single-engine planes—all of them owned and operated by business concerns or private individuals —and on that ideal spring day, many of them were up.

It was the first time I had ever been on a private airport and I confess that the blood began to pound in my veins at the sight of the brightly colored airplanes all around us, parked in lines like so many cars in a parking lot.

The field, washed in warm sunshine, was a beehive of activity. The line crew, dressed in coveralls with the word "Wings" inscribed across their backs, was rushing around, busily untying tie-down ropes, turning over propellers and helping people with luggage.

I saw planes being hauled in and out of large hangars and taxied along the macadam taxiways out to the hard twenty-six-hundred-foot main runway, where they queued up for take-off, one after the other, like children waiting their turn on a sliding board.

Adjacent to the operations building was the Philadelphia Aviation Country Club, with an old clubhouse, outdoor patio, bar, tennis courts, just like any other country club, except that it is used by aviators rather than golfers, and the language seems somewhat more temperate.

I could see and hear sun-tanned youngsters cavorting in the club swimming pool not two hundred feet away, while the air around us was filled with the angry buzzing of light-plane engines taking off, landing or just flying around.

Over everything was the distinct feeling of an outing, the same feeling you have when you spread a blanket in the country for an old-fashioned picnic. Everything was easy and relaxed, with lots of laughing and good-natured banter. Something creaked inside my skull again. This I liked!

Tom clamped down on my arm as he pointed to a small yellow plane coming in for a landing.

"There's Bob now," he said excitedly, and we both began to wave like a couple of yokels in a television audience.

In a moment Bob taxied a trim little Piper Pacer up to the gate and beckoned us to get in. I ducked under the wing, opened the door and slid into the right front seat beside Bob. Tom hopped into the back seat, performing a hurried introduction. With that, the engine roared and off we went, bouncing and jouncing across the sod.

I noticed that there was no wheel on my side, and was glad, because I was afraid I might grab the controls and "freeze" to them, as I had read somewhere in some old books, and ram us into the ground. Oh, my! I was just full of ideas like that. I had a lot to learn.

As we began our take-off run into the wind, I suddenly became tense and apprehensive, because not only am I the kind of a guy who suffers from vertigo on a high curb, I am also prone to motion sickness on a ferry boat. If you get seasick on a boat, you have a rail—in the plane I had only my lap. I shuddered slightly and opened the ventilators as the plane gathered speed over the ground. I also tried hard to figure out some way to stop it so I could get out. "This is not for me," I thought, "it's all a mistake." Then suddenly the ground fell away from us and we were airborne.

I had built myself up to a big letdown. There was no breath-taking feeling of ascent such as you get in an elevator. It was more as if the world had dropped away and left the plane and its occupants suspended in the air, dangling on a string like a populated yoyo.

And I was even more surprised at the fact that there was no feeling of height, of dizziness or vertigo. I felt no different than I did sitting in a car looking down at the street, except that there, fifteen hundred feet below us, were tiny houses and cars and people. And the motion was most agreeable.

Nothing was real from up there; it was like being transported to another world. The world I knew was gone, as I saw it in a new perspective. I couldn't see the dirt of the streets, or the cracked paint on the houses, or the worried expressions on the faces of the people down below. Up there it was clean and free and beautiful. The landscape spread out like a patchwork quilt, and gossamer wisps of cloud drifted past under us. I was literally in heaven.

When Bob cut the throttle and began to lose altitude to land, I felt a definite twinge of regret that it had to end so quickly; that we had to return to the world of houses needing paint and streets needing cleaning, and people with worried expressions. Then we were bumping along the grass and turning toward the open door of the big hangar alongside the field.

We climbed out of the Pacer and were greeted by the airport manager, the owner of the 140 I had come to see.

"Where is she?" I asked. The owner nodded sideways with his head toward the dim recesses of the man-made cave, and I saw for the first time Cessna seven three zero four four.

There she sat, all by herself, back in the far corner of the hangar, forlorn and sad. The little silver airplane reminded me of an orphan waiting to be adopted from a drab asylum. I had an immediate flush of affection for the plane; it was love at first sight, as they say in the pulp magazines.

We wheeled her out into the late afternoon sunlight and Bob went over her from nose to tail—squinting, craning, peering, thumping, shaking, like a physician tending a patient. Then he leafed through the log books with a practiced eye, and after a while, as the owner and I stood there in the warm sun watching, he took her around the field and brought her back to a gentle landing, like a perfectly cast dry fly on a small stream.

By way of small talk, I asked the owner, "How much do you want?" expecting him to come back with "Oh, twenty-five-hundred bucks," so we could haggle. He squinted his eyes at the little plane as it rolled toward us over the grass and hesitated for a moment.

"I won't take a cent less than fifteen hundred dollars," he said, sucking on a match stick. "I really don't want to sell it, but I need the hangar space."

I was rocked back on my heels. $1500! That was not as much as I had intended to pay, and it left $500 for operating expenses and lessons. Then a fear arose in my mind. Maybe the plane was a lemon!

I walked over to the 140 as Bob cut the ignition and climbed out.

"Is it any good?" I asked doubtfully. He looked at me directly and jabbed a cigarette in his mouth.

"If I had the dough, I'd buy it myself." That settled that.

"Will you teach me how to fly it?" I asked.

"Sure," he said with a grin, and that settled that. I was a goner. My new car and my wife's mink stole went out the window as my skull really creaked.

I turned to the owner. "If you will have the plane and a bill of sale at Wings Field next Wednesday afternoon, I will have a certified check in the amount of one thousand, five hundred dollars for you."

"O. K.," he said. So he did. So I did. So I bought this airplane.

2.   Bethlehem

As you may well imagine, I went home to my wife that Wednesday with uneasy stirrings of my conscience, after permanently warping the family budget by shelling out a sizable hunk of cash for an airplane I didn't know how to fly. As I handed over the certified check I had felt, like the girl in the story, that I was going to hate myself in the morning.

No matter how slowly I tried to drive, I finally reached home.

Then, with my family gathered around me, I launched into a halting recitation of the facts surrounding the purchase. The three boys were on my side, all right, but my frau absorbed the news with hard-eyed reserve—an ominous silence. So the instant I had a chance I excused myself, telephoned Bob Angeli and extracted from him the promise that he would start instructing me the very next morning, before I went cold on the whole project. Stone cold.

By 8:15 A.M. the next day, I was sitting alone in the tied-down 140 working the slack controls and wondering what it would be like up there among the fleecy clouds

—something like a fourteen-year-old boy in his father's car, pretending he had his driver's license.

By nine o'clock I was growing apprehensive. Maybe Bob had forgotten our date. But even as I fretted, a Ford sedan snaked into the driveway and out stepped jaunty Robert with a dazzling smile.

After we shook hands (mine cold and clammy, his warm and dry), we got right down to business.

"An airplane is to fly," Bob said, "but *each* time before it is flown, it must be checked."

Up to that time the word "checked" meant leaving my fedora in the hands of some nice-looking young lady when I entered a public place, so I asked him what he meant.

"Well," he said, rolling an unlighted cigarette from one corner of his mouth to the other with a deft flick of his tongue—a trick which I have often admired but never can duplicate—"if you are going trout fishing, you certainly look to be sure that there are no holes in your waders before you get into the stream; otherwise you might wind up with wet feet. That's the way it is with an airplane. Before you go into the sky you examine your plane; otherwise you may wind up with *flat* feet. . . . Flat everything," he added darkly, as an afterthought. If he had meant to scare me, he sure as hell succeeded.

"G'by," I said, and started for the car.

Bob grabbed my belt, hauled me back and handed me a five-by-seven card mounted in plastic. On the card were printed instructions entitled "Check List."

"Let's run through this," he said, pointing to the first section, which was marked "Ground Check."

In this check-off, we started at the nose of the plane and went all the way around it in a clockwise direction.

First we examined the propeller for nicks, gouges and bends. It was as smooth as a tot's tokus. Bob took the prop in both hands and shook it, hard. He twisted it one way and then the other, listening all the while for the metallic clicking sounds which, he explained, might indicate a loose connection or a worn bearing. No clicks, thank heaven!

On the front of the propeller hub were six bolts which held the prop on the plane. The heads of these bolts had holes drilled in them perpendicular to the body of the bolt, and all of the bolts were then connected by a strong wire running through these holes; that way the bolts can't unscrew themselves and allow the prop to whirl off into space on its own, which makes the engine race and disconcerts the occupants. The wire was in good shape. I wasn't!

Then we opened the right side of the hood, or "cowling," and examined all the spark plugs, wires, screws and fittings. The oil level was checked by means of a dip stick similar to the one in my car. I was thankful that something looked familiar.

We drained a cupful of gas out of the carburetor sediment bowl to be sure no water or dirt would get into the carburetor and do something naughty to the engine.

Speaking of the engine, an eighty-five-horsepower Continental (C-85), I was considerably surprised to see how little it was compared to the rest of the plane. It made me wonder.

Then we closed and firmly latched the cowling and moved to the right wing, which we examined for wrinkles, soft spots and holes in the fabric. Until that moment I hadn't even noticed that the wings were fabric-covered. I had thought that they were metal, like the fuselage. Bob seized the very tip of the wing and rocked the plane to see if there was any play or looseness in the structure. Everything was tight, especially my stomach.

We examined the ailerons and their hinges, the rudder, the elevators and their hinges, and the flaps and *their* hinges, checked the gas tanks to be sure they were filled, and finally arrived back at the nose of the airplane, as the surveyors say, at "the first mentioned point and place of beginning."

Oh yes, we also examined the landing gear. There isn't much to examine on Cessna landing gear, because it is simply two pieces of spring steel, but with the tires— well, I have been a tire-kicker since away back when I first started driving cars. So when Bob got through examining the fat little tires on the 140 for cuts and bruises, and kicked them to test their inflation, I followed suit. Made me feel better. This I understood.

At last the time arrived to get into the plane. In deference to Bob's position as instructor, I started to get in the right seat, knowing from reading *Flying* that the left seat is where the pilot sits.

"Hey," said Bob, "this is your airplane, *you* sit on the left." I slid into the left-hand seat, although I felt pretty self-conscious.

"How am I ever going to learn all of these things?" I asked, nodding at the dial-studded instrument panel.

"Forget them right now," he answered offhandedly, fastening his seat belt. I followed his example and ran my web belt snug across my lap. This quickly becomes habitual in a plane, and I now do it automatically, even if I am only going to taxi to the gas pit, or sit in the plane to listen to the radio.

Bob told me to go through section two of the check

list: "Before Starting Engine." I ran my eye down the list and read aloud as Bob pointed out the location of the appropriate gadgets.

"*Fuel 'on,' both tanks,*" I read, and reached for the tank-selector valve down by my right knee.

"This doesn't have 'both' on it," Bob said, "but the later models do. Put it in the left tank." I did as he told me.

"*Set brakes.*"

He leaned over and peered at the floor. "I have no brakes on my side, so I'll have to depend on you," he said.

"*Mixture full rich,*" I read.

"This has no mixture control either," said Bob, squinting at the panel. I began to wonder if the plane was complete.

"*Set clock,*" I read, and swung the hands on the eight-day clock in front of me.

"*Flaps up.*" O. K.

"*Set altimeter, . . .* where to?" I asked.

Bob pointed to the sign on the flight office. "Wings Field 330 feet," and I ran the pointer on the instrument to 330.

"*Controls free.*" I looked at Bob and raised my eyebrows.

"All that means is, roll the wheel and pedals to be sure that everything works, and to check that you haven't forgotten to take off any wedges or locks put on the control surfaces to keep them from blowing in a gusty wind while the plane is tied down." I had been doing this since eight-fifteen, but did it again anyhow. Everything was O. K.

Bob was sitting there looking at me as I hesitated. "Well, go ahead, Dad," he said impatiently.

Section three: *Starting Engine*. A shiver went up my spine.

"Set brakes," I said. O. K.

"Turn on master switch." Click, it was on.

"Crack throttle." That one stopped me. Bob smiled, reached for the doorknob-like black ball extending from the long stem at the bottom of the panel and pulled it all the way out.

"Throttle closed," he said. He pushed it about half an inch into the panel. "Throttle 'cracked.' Go ahead."

"Turn on magneto switches." I looked where Bob pointed to two toggle switches side by side marked "left" and "right," and snapped them both to the "on" position.

"Open the window and yell 'Clear,'" ordered the professor, and I did so, good and loud.

"Press starter button."

"On this plane, you pull a knob," said Bob, pointing to the left side of the panel, where a flattened knob was marked "Starter." I pulled the knob tentatively. Immediately the silence of the cabin was shattered by a mechanical grinding noise that picked up in tempo three times. "RRRRRRR-RRRRRRR-RRRRRRR," then a loud "BROOOOOOOM," as the engine surged into life, dropping back to a nice idle "Pocketa-pocketa-pocketa."

I thought of Walter Mitty. "Pocketa-pocketa-pocketa."

The tachometer needle moved from o to about 800 rpm and stayed there, vibrating slightly. Bob put his right index finger on the glass of the oil-pressure gauge and spoke over the ticking of the engine.

"If this needle doesn't register any pressure within twenty seconds, cut the switch." I counted slowly to myself, eying the needle closely; it was still on o. At "ten" the needle suddenly broke loose and jumped to 45 pounds.

"Now listen," said Bob, half turning toward me with his left arm along the top of the seat behind my back. "On a still day like this you steer airplanes on the ground with your feet only. Leave the wheel alone, it has no effect. Put your heels on the floor with just your toes on the pedals, push the left pedal forward and give her a little gas."

I gingerly pushed the throttle knob and the C-85 up front snarled as we moved forward a few feet, then swung left down the taxi strip.

The sound of taxiing the 140 with its metal fuselage reminded me of an old jungle-type moving picture I had seen years before, where there was a deep ceaseless booming from all around, and an Englishman with a monocle and cork hat observed, "The natives are restless tonight." On the rolling turf, the booming of the fuselage almost drowned out the engine. "Pocketa-pocketa-*boom-boom*-pocketa."

As we taxied down the field, Bob made me keep swinging—first left, then right—in a zigzag course, so that we could see past the high nose to be sure there were no holes or rocks in our path. Because of this zigzagging, or because my vision to the right was blocked by the nose-high position of the plane on the ground, or something, our path down the field was not straight. Instead, I gradually worked our way over to the right edge, along which there was an apple orchard, whose gnarled trees were fully capable of tearing the fabric off the right wing, if not bending the wing itself.

"Yikes! Turn *left*, Frank!" yelled Bob, and my automobile reflexes, conditioned by twenty years of driving experience that said, "To go left turn the wheel left," had me wrenching the control wheel hard over, which had no effect on the airplane's course toward the outreaching branches.

"Stop!" yelled Bob, and another automobile reflex took over.

In a car emergency, my right foot, normally on the accelerator pedal, moves about six inches to the left to the brake pedal and jabs at it to stop the car. When Bob yelled "Stop!" my right foot automatically moved off the right rudder-and-brake pedal and smashed down savagely on the left rudder-and-brake pedal six inches to the left—and incidentally, on the toes of my left foot. The left brake locked, the plane pivoted suddenly out of danger, with only inches to spare, and Bob congratulated me for quick thinking.

I didn't have the nerve to tell him how the sudden turn actually came about. Those toes hurt me for a week!

In a few minutes we were parked at a forty-five-degree-angle near the end of the runway and running through Check List sections 4 and 5: "Warm Up" and "Take Off."

The oil pressure was still at 45 pounds, the needles of the oil-temperature and cylinder-head-temperature gauges were both "in the green." O. K.

I opened the throttle until the tachometer read 1600 rpm and as directed, turned off first the left, then the right magneto. The rpm's dropped to 1575 on the left and 1550 on the right, but Bob said a drop of seventy-five rpm was permissible on either mag, so everything was jake. Personally, I didn't know what I was doing.

At his instruction I pulled out on knob marked "carburetor heat" and saw the rpm's drop to 1500 then I pushed it in and saw the rpm's build up again. I looked at Bob in wonder.

"Don't worry," he said, the way I talk to my small children when they ask where babies come from, "I'll explain it to you later." He was running his practiced eye over the panel and its vibrating needles, then he leaned over and glanced all around at the skyline.

"O. K.," he said suddenly, "let's go. Point her into the wind and gradually open the throttle all the way." In sort of a daze, I did as he told me.

"After all," I thought, "he will take over the controls as soon as we get rolling."

But as the C-85 wound up in a crescendo of power and the propeller flailed the air, he didn't make a move toward the wheel. We began to roll faster and faster, and still he sat there, apparently relaxed and comfortable as the Continental's eighty-five horses pranced in their traces ahead of us and the plane bounced and boomed across the ground. I was hanging onto the wheel, which had suddenly become alive in my hands, wondering when the whole thing was going to blow up.

"All right," said Bob, as he leaned slightly toward me so his voice was clear in my right ear, "push forward on the wheel a little." I did, and the nose came down level so I could see the grass stretching out ahead of us.

"Now ease back a little," said Bob. Despite the racket from the wide-open engine, I was surprised to find that we could converse easily. No speaking tube needed! I tugged gently at the wheel, and as if by magic, the bouncing stopped—we were flying. *I* was flying! As Bob told me what to do, I maintained a rate of climb at seventy-five miles per hour until we were four hundred feet above the ground (the altimeter read 730), then he "talked me" into a left turn. He looked behind me out of the little side window to see where the runway was.

"A lousy turn and not ninety degrees from the strip," he said, "but we'll fix that."

Under Bob's directions I made a few level turns, and climbing turns, and eventually the altimeter read 1900. He pointed to the little magnetic compass in the center of the panel.

"Put this on three hundred fifty-nine and keep it there. We might as well get you an I. D. card and student's license."

"Where do you get them?" I asked, thinking, for some reason, of North Philadelphia Airport, and trying to figure why the compass moved around so skittishly—and wondering which way 359 was, anyhow.

"Bethlehem," he answered casually, lighting a cigarette and turning the ventilator in the windshield to suck the smoke out of the cabin. One moment a blue haze hung there, the next, woosh! it was whisked out of that little hole in the side of the plexiglass.

Bethlehem! It finally hit me. That's a hundred-mile round trip, a two-hour car ride each way, most of the times I have made it. And we had no maps, no navigation instruments, no radio charts!

"The man is mad," I thought, growing damp between the shoulder blades. And I clutched the wheel until the knuckles of both hands showed white; yet there sat Bob, his left foot propped up on the little shelf in front of the seat, a cigarette hanging carelessly from the fingers of his left hand which was resting on his raised knee, idly gazing down at the limitless carpet of green, brown and black squares, oblongs and triangles sliding past under our wings.

"Look at that, Frank," he said, exhaling a haze of smoke and nodding at the earth below. "Thousands of landing fields as far as the eye can see. I'll teach you how to get down into them safely."

Suddenly he stumped his cigarette out in the ash tray.

"Look at your white knuckles." I looked at the death grip I had on the wheel. "Just what are you afraid of?" he asked. "Too many people think flying is hard—it's not. This plane doesn't need you, anyhow. Take your hands off the wheel." I let go of the controls, but kept my hands poised to seize them immediately if the nose went up or down suddenly. The little plane continued to fly along on a slightly undulating course, rolling up and down on the invisible air currents, like a small boat in a long ground swell.

"Y'see," he said, "the plane can fly itself better than you can fly it. Now push the left pedal."

I pushed it gingerly, hands still off the wheel, and the little plane set itself in a gentle bank, turning to the left. I pushed the right pedal and we went into a right turn.

"Take the wheel and remove your feet from the pedals," Bob ordered. "Now bank her to the left." I turned the wheel to the left. Immediately the left wing dropped, but the nose first swung to the right in a yaw before it began to come left into a turn.

"That is caused by aileron drag. Look out the window at the trailing edge of the wing," said Bob, as he leaned over in front of me to peer out the left side. He twisted the wheel right and I saw the aileron on my side come down at a sharp angle. He twisted the wheel left and the aileron went up, but not quite as far in its travel.

"When you want to pick a wing up by deflecting the aileron down on that side, remember that the depressed aileron acts as a flap, and drags the wing back on that side, and you will get a yaw." Thus I learned that the rudder is used, not to turn the plane, but to prevent the yaw caused by aileron drag on the wing going up. That is why you must use the wheel (or stick) and rudder together; every time you move one you must move the other. "Coordinated controls," they call it.

There are, I also learned, four instruments called the "flight group" which are interrelated and are directly affected by the action of the controls: the needle (turn indicator), the ball (bank indicator), the airspeed indicator and the altimeter (altitude indicator). These instruments are the primary ones used for blind flying—flying when the pilot cannot see the ground and has no reference points to tell him visually what the attitude of the plane is in the air.

The needle is affected by the rudder pedals. If you push the left pedal the plane will turn left and the needle will lean to the left.

The ball is associated with the needle and shows whether the turn is properly banked, not being skidded or slipped—a very important thing to know, especially at slow speeds. These two instruments make sense and are easily understood.

The airspeed indicator, of course, tells how fast the airplane is going through the air, and the altimeter tells how high it is; but they tell something else too, and that's where the learning process comes in: the airspeed is controlled by the stick or wheel, the control that inclines the plane up or down. If you are cruising at one hundred twenty miles per hour and want to slow down, you ease back on the stick and the airspeed will fall back. If you ease forward on the stick, the nose will drop and the airspeed will build up. The altimeter is affected by the use of the throttle: if you want to climb, you give the engine more gas; if you want to descend, you retard the throttle —in both cases you maintain a constant airspeed by the stick.

This is the part of flying that is completely new to such novices as I was then. Like most people, I had always thought that the wheel made you go up and down and the throttle made you go fast or slow. This was fun!

Bob told me this stuff was called "air work," and I practiced all the way to Bethlehem, weaving through the air like a drunken eagle: stick and rudder left, turn left; stick and rudder right, turn right. Keep it straight and level. Open throttle: climb two hundred feet. Retard throttle: descend a hundred feet.

And stalls. The word "stall" has always frightened me and, like a dope, I mentioned it to Bob.

"Pull on the carburetor heat," he said, by way of answer. "Make a ninety-degree left and a ninety-degree right turn to clear the air." I made the turns, although I wasn't sure what he had meant about clearing the air. "Now cut the throttle back to idle." I did so.

"Pull back on the wheel." I pulled the wheel and the nose went up, up, up, the stall warning indicator went "beep—beep—beeeeeeeeep" and the controls went soft, then mushy, then slack.

"Let go of the wheel," said Bob and, when I did the

nose dropped and the earth appeared over the nose as the 140 slid into a gentle left turn.

"O. K., level her out," said Bob. "*That*, me boy, was a 'stall.' The airplane recovered itself, because it is built to do so. As long as you don't hold the wheel back too far you will never stall. If you do feel a stall, push the wheel forward and pick up flying speed.

"Let's do a few more, but don't let go of the wheel. Fly it through the stall and the recovery." So, as he instructed me, I punched another bogy man full of holes. The things that I had been so afraid of were all in my imagination, it seemed, and I have a helluva lively imagination!

Not once did Bob touch the controls. He would say, "Pull the wheel back and hold it there." The nose would come up and the airspeed would fall back, and the wheel would get heavier and heavier in my hands, and the stall buzzer would sound off. Then, just as the controls went all mushy, he would tell me to push the wheel forward and feed her the juice, and in a flash the nose would come down and the airspeed would build up again and she flew under full control. We did power-on and power-off stalls, ten or fifteen in all. I wondered what people on the ground thought about the peculiar antics of the plane overhead.

Then Bob reached across in front of me, picked the microphone off the hook and turned the radio on to the "Comm" position. He rotated the control until the pointer came to the place on the dial marked "T, 278 KC," on the communications band.

As the radio warmed up he put the headset on over his ears and then pushed the microphone button and held the unit up to his lips. I had seen this done in the movies but hadn't the slightest idea of what he was saying. I began peering out of the windows to see where we were, but I couldn't make anything out except some tiny houses, a river and lots of smoke and haze. Suddenly the headphones were slid down over my ears from behind and I heard a metallic voice speaking:

"Zero four four cleared to land immediately; right turn in, Runway six, altimeter setting three zero zero one, Wind five."

Bob yelled, "That's you. Tell him 'Roger,'" and slipped the microphone into my hand. I didn't know to whom I was telling "Roger," why I was telling him "Roger," or what I was saying "Roger" to, but I dutifully pressed the microphone button, put the mike to my lips and said, "Roger."

Bob then took over the controls and dropped the right wing in a fast descending turn. As he did so, I looked out my left window and saw two big twin-engined planes, one behind the other, about two miles away, coming straight at us. Just then Bob said, "O. K., you have it." I thought that it was a ridiculous time for me to "have it," with those big planes heading right at us, but when I looked ahead through the windshield, there was a beautiful, dead-end, ten-lane highway stretching out a mile ahead of me, flat as a billiard table. My first landing was to be at a large airport! I tensed up, but Bob was again relaxed and talking in my right ear.

"Watch the airspeed, keep it at 75. Pull the nose up a little. There, that's it. See the airspeed drop to 70? Don't use the flaps, just hold her right there." Even I could see that the runway was coming up closer and closer at what seemed to be blinding speed.

"Back just a little," he said. The airspeed dropped to 65. "A little more"—60, then 55, then a quick "beeeeep" on the stall-warning indicator as the lift bled out of the wing, and we settled onto the ground at about the same speed I usually drive my car.

As Bob instructed me we turned right, off the runway to a taxi strip and the voice in the headphones said, "Very nice, zero four four, thank you for clearing the 'active' so fast." It made me feel good—like a smile from a pretty girl.

When we got out of the plane in front of the FAA office, I looked at my watch—thirty-one minutes since leaving Wings! No traffic, no honking, no snarling drivers, no rush, and no stop lights.

I climbed the steps to the FAA office, filled out some papers and got a card describing me as an "Airman." I turned to Bob and asked, "How the hell did I get into this?"

His grin answered mine. "Welcome, birdman," he said.

I don't remember the trip back to Wings. In fact, I suspect that I didn't fly in the 140 at all. I rode all the way home on Cloud Number Six.

3. Ups and Downs

As millions of students have done before me, and millions will do when I am gone, I spent most of my first eight hours of basic training going around and around a rectangular pattern, practicing take-offs, turns, approaches and landings.

Every time it was the same, and yet it was different. Take off, climb to four hundred feet, level off, throttle back, turn left ninety degrees, climb to six hundred feet, turn left ninety degrees to eight hundred feet; carburetor heat on, throttle to idle, turn ninety degrees left onto base leg, then another ninety degrees left to final approach; land. Taxi back and do it all over again. And again. And again.

For me the most difficult hurdle while learning to fly was unlearning habits that had been developed over many years from a pattern of past, non-flying experiences, especially those connected with automobiles. Because I have been driving cars for twenty years, I have developed certain definite convictions about their behavior. One is that a car operates better on a smooth, paved highway than it does on a beach or a golf course.

Another is that, as soon as a car stops "tracking" at high speed, that is, the rear wheels stop following the front ones, there is a great likelihood that the car is going to turn over.

Since the cabins of modern, light planes are so much like the inside of our cars, these two ideas are very persistent when you first start to fly. You think that smooth, paved runways are the best ones to operate from, yet it is really easier on the plane and its tires to land on grass, even on a rough field.

When I first started to make cross-wind take-offs and landings, this car-conditioned reflex scared me, because as we began to roll and gather speed, and therefore develop lift in the wings, I noticed frequently that we were bouncing across the grass at a heading off our course, or a "crab angle," like a skid in a car, and I was afraid that we were going to turn over and strike a wing tip. I told Angeli of my fear.

Bob opened the throttle and, as we roared over the grass, kicked the rudder first one way, then the other, so that the 140 slewed around almost thirty degrees in each direction; but the wings stayed level with the ground, and we took off without trouble. The wheels slide on grass!

And we landed on fields that I wouldn't ride a tractor over, much less a car, but the Cessna landing gear didn't have any trouble at all. The spring-steel gear flexed and absorbed the shock, and in the cabin we didn't feel it at all. I don't think you can hurt Cessna gear. It is built to take the roughest treatment, without suffering any ill effects.

But Bob's approach had changed. Now, when I made a mistake, he let me have it with both barrels; a slipped or a skidded turn brought forth a tirade. Most of the time it seemed he yelled at me *before* I made a mistake, which is even faster than my wife operates, after years of practice.

I would cut the throttle and turn onto base leg.

"Watch your airspeed," he would grate. Then I would turn onto final approach, when the timing is more critical.

"Watch your airspeed, goddamnit!" he would snarl, and I would move the wheel gently to keep the airspeed at 70—back wheel to slow up, forward to pick up speed.

"You're too high!" he would scold halfway to the runway. The engine would roar and around I would go to make a correct approach. Once in a while I completed the circuit without his saying a word. Once in a long while. To this day I can still hear his yell, "Watch your airspeed," when I cut the gun to make a landing.

Airspeed is to an airplane the same thing a heartbeat is to you and me. As long as you have it you are able to go along on an even keel, but the moment you lose it, down you go.

There is an old maxim among pilots to the effect that altitude is insurance. That is only another way of saying that if something goes wrong you can use the force of gravity to develop airspeed and regain positive control. But airspeed is really the insurance, and altitude is merely the premium, because "lift" and airspeed are two inseparable physical conditions; so long as you have airspeed you have lift and control; when you lose your airspeed you lose your lift just like a skipping stone that slows down and sinks into the water, and woosh, down you go until you can build up airspeed and lift again. Close to the ground, you have no altitude, no money in the bank, and if you lose too much airspeed in an approach and, therefore, lose your lift, you may stall the plane right into the ground before you reach the edge of the field, dead-broke. Certainly broke, and maybe dead. Therefore, for practice, each landing is made "dead-stick" or without power, simulating emergency landings when you won't have power to go around again. All you have is your St. Christopher's medal to see you down safely.

We almost wore a rectangular hole in the sky as I learned to keep my airspeed and rate of descent and all of the other things under control, like a juggler who must keep several eggs in the air at once. When I first started, I had to think of every move I made; but if I forgot something, there was Bob to let me know about it— loud and clear.

"Come *on*, Frank," he would say. "Fly it *right!*" And he would mutter to himself, fold his arms across his chest and glower out the window. It made me feel terrible.

I learned to juggle. If the nose dropped too far, the airspeed would build up from 70 to 80 and I would have a long floating flare-out before the airspeed dropped enough for me to sit her down on the ground. So I would hold the nose high and keep the airspeed constant, with intense concentration, and finally began to come in fairly nicely on my landings, although I was still dependent on my airspeed indicator to tell what I should do on final approach. Even I could note the improvement and Bob told me I was "getting there." It gave me confidence, like a friendly expression on the face of a juror while you are making a closing speech.

One morning when I arrived at the field I noticed that Bob was already out on the line taking the seat cushions out of the 140 and putting them in the back seat of his car.

As I approached him he looked up with his characteristic grin, said, "Here y'are, Dad, put this on," and handed me a bulky, seat-type parachute. A vague fear crossed my mind.

"What's the big idea?" I asked, trying to sound fairly unafraid, and failing dismally.

"Spins today," he answered laconically, "and the FAA requires chutes—just in case." This last, darkly, with lowered brows. Sort of a dirty trick, considering my delicate condition. "Puckered stomach," I think they call it.

I looked the chute over from all sides and developed a doubt that I could get the thing on at all, much less get it on so it would stay on. Wouldn't it be awful to jump out in a parachute, pull the rip cord and have the empty chute drift to earth long after the jumper had arrived "sans impedimenta"? I felt as if I were in the clutches of a moldy octopus with those web straps all over me.

"Oh, for heaven's sakes," said Bob, "put those two gizmos over your shoulders and pull your arms through here." He indicated the shoulder and waist straps.

He snapped a clasp just over my heart, which was doing a fast mambo, and pointed to the pull ring.

"If you have to jump, hang onto this," he said. "Otherwise you have to pay three bucks for a new one."

Yes, I'm *sure* they call it "puckered stomach."

The seat pack was now hanging down behind me at a peculiar angle, with the lower edge pressing against the backs of my knees.

"Get in the plane," said Bob, "and we can fasten the leg straps."

Get in the plane—ha! I could hardly walk with that thing on, and being a fairly big guy I have to scrunch down a little to get into the 140 under the best of conditions. So when it came time to try to get in with that bulky pack on my behind, I couldn't make it alone. With the help of two of the line crew, I finally backed into the seat, and with much wiggling and squirming finally got turned around in the right direction. When Bob got into the plane he was wiping tears from his eyes, but I didn't think it was that funny.

Besides, I wondered if all those gymnastics had done anything to disconnect the controls of the chute. I shuddered slightly, fastened the leg straps, ran through the check list and took off, but my heart wasn't in it.

As we climbed to thirty-five hundred feet, I became aware that my shirt was dripping wet from perspiration. I mentioned it to Bob.

"Oh, that's just nervous tension," he said, lighting a cigarette as the altimeter passed 2000 feet. "Everyone is afraid of spins before they do them. Actually a spin is a rotating descending stall and is a very useful maneuver for losing altitude quickly. You won't have any trouble; in fact, I'm going to let you do the whole thing yourself.

"Head her over there," he said, pointing to a clear area over some open farm land, "and level off at thirty-five hundred feet."

He half turned toward me in his characteristic side-saddle position, with his left arm along the back of my seat.

"You have done lots of stalls and know how to recover from them. Now you are going to carry through the stall and spin pattern. When I tell you, cut the en-

gine and pull her up into a stall. When you feel her go
'mushy' and lose lateral control, don't let the wheel go
forward, hold it *all* the way back and *kick* the left rudder hard. When she has done a couple of turns, release
the wheel a little, give her opposite rudder a hard kick
to stop the spin and level off. Nothing to it."

He looked around to see where we were, and told
me to make "clearing turns," which I had learned were
nothing more than a ninety-degree left followed by a
ninety-degree right to let other aircraft in the vicinity
know that we were going to enter some radical maneuver. I felt as if I were about to be hung.

"O. K.," he said, reaching for the lighter in the panel,
"spin her to the left a couple of times." He used the
same tone he might have used to say, "Looks like rain
tonight."

I pulled on the carburetor heat and closed the throttle. Immediately the nose wanted to drop, but I pulled
back on the growing-heavy wheel. The stall warning indicator set up a steady "beeeeeeep" until Bob leaned
over and snapped off the master switch. The nose was
pointing up at a crazy angle and all I could see was blue
sky and a few wisps of cloud past the slowly revolv-
ing propeller. The airspeed dropped rapidly—100
. . . 90 . . . 80 . . . 50 . . . 40—and she shuddered
slightly as if she had a chill—the stall! Instead of re-
leasing the back pressure of the wheel, as I had done
many times before, I held the wheel against my chest
and shoved hard on the left pedal. The left wing
dropped, and in a flash we flicked over on our back in a
twisting, turning dive. For an instant I saw the crazy-
quilt pattern of farms through the blue-tinted skylights
over my head; then I saw them in front of me, revolv-

ing rapidly in a clockwise direction. I eased the wheel forward and fed in a little right rudder. The spin stopped, and we were in a steep dive.

"Now back a little," said Bob, and suddenly we were straight and level at twenty-five hundred feet.

"That wasn't so bad, now, was it?" he asked, as the engine roared again. His arm was still across the back of my seat. I nodded, but couldn't seem to get my teeth unclenched.

"Do it again to the right," he ordered as we climbed slowly back to thirty-five hundred feet.

I thought back to the winter days when I was a kid with a sled. We would skim down the hill in a few seconds, then trudge up the hill slowly to get another short ride. Same thing with spins. Down quick, slow back.

When we got back to the top of the hill, Bob warned me, "It's a lot harder to spin to the right, so hold it back and kick her over as if you meant it!"

He fished another cigarette out of his pocket as I pulled on the carb heat and cut the throttle. Out of the corner of my eye I saw him reaching for the lighter on the panel as we pulled up into the stall and, as we went over on our back he was calmly lighting his cigarette. My shirt was beginning to dry out. This was easy!

On my second spin to the right, a funny thing happened. I stalled her out and gave her right rudder. However, instead of going into a tailspin, she dropped her right wing, her nose swung down and we went into a lazy spiral to the right. I couldn't figure it out, and looked at Bob with a quizzical expression.

"That's what happens when you don't hold the wheel far enough back to keep it stalled out. The wing drops, the plane falls sideways and builds up airspeed, and you go into a descending turn. You will never spin unless you hold the wheel all the way back. Remember that for later, Dad."

We did a few more spins and recoveries, and headed for home, fat and sassy.

"Let's see how slowly this thing will fly," said Bob, as we headed back towards Wings at two thousand feet. Little by little I eased back on the throttle, at the same time maintaining altitude with the elevators.

Finally the tachometer needle was wavering around 1600 rpm, the airspeed was 48 mph—and still we flew, nose high, "mushing" through the atmosphere. As we wallowed along just one wing would drop, then the other, and Bob taught me to bring up the low wing with a short, sharp push on the opposite rudder pedal.

"At low speed the wing is almost stalled out. When a wing drops it means that that wing is more stalled out than the other. If you try to pick it up with the aileron, the depressed aileron, as you know, will act as a flap and create drag so that the wing stalls out completely and you will go into a spin or a tight spiral. In 'slow flight,' when you give it opposite rudder, you swing the low wing ahead, so that the two wings become balanced again. If you ever have a partial engine failure and get down to sixteen hundred rpm's, you can still fly it home—if you don't get scared."

We opened her up to 2350 rpm, the normal cruise, and trimmed for 110 mph.

Suddenly, the engine coughed and died! I reached for the throttle knob and my fingers came to rest over the tanned hand of my instructor, who had cut the throttle to idle.

"Where are you going to land it?" he asked sharply. "Which way is the wind blowing?" I was completely off balance mentally and started to stutter out an answer.

Bob snapped at me. "You should *always* know the direction of the wind on the ground! Look for smoke from factories or chimneys or brush fires. Watch for flags, wash on a line, or ripples on large bodies of water. You must be sure to land into the wind, or the plane just keeps on rolling along, like Ol' Man River, until you hit something solid. Keep your eyes peeled all the time for a place to set her down—pastures, super-highways, golf courses—anywhere that the ground is not too rough or the grass too high, because that will put you over on your back. Remember, for every thousand feet of altitude you have, you can glide about ten thousand feet in almost any direction; from five thousand feet you have your pick of three hundred square miles to land on. That's a lot of real estate, Dad. Somewhere it *has* to be flat!"

All the time Bob was talking to me, I was trying to line up to get into a plowed field, and had the flaps down ready to land. Then he opened the throttle and we roared up under full power to a safe altitude.

Back at Wings Field, Bob taught me how to sideslip to lose altitude quickly and safely to get into a small space in case of an emergency.

Sideslipping gives you a funny feeling when you first start, because you turn the wheel one way, say to the left, to make a left slip, and push the pedals the other way, that is, to the right, and the airplane cocks itself over so you see the runway coming up at you from the side of the nose, then you let her straighten out and, swish, you are down. Learning to ride the bicycle again.

Bob made me do six slips from each side, and when we finally landed, I knew I had done a hard day's work. I wasn't too sure of my theory, but felt that I could handle the plane pretty well by myself now, and told Bob so. You might say I was confused, but confident. Bob just looked at me strangely for a moment.

The next day, as we taxied out for take-off, he began to tape a large piece of brown wrapping paper over the instrument panel. We ran through the check-off at the end of the runway; then Bob taped over the tachometer, and sat back in his seat with a smug look on his face, like a man who has just successfully set up a hot foot and is waiting for the victim to feel it.

"All right, Hot Pilot," he said amiably, "let's see how good you are without the crutches."

With a flourish, I opened the throttle and pointed her down the runway. We began rolling faster and faster, bouncing and swaying as the prop bit into the air. I got the tail up and then hauled back on the wheel. "Beeeeeeep" went the stall-warning indicator as we lurched into the air. Whoops! Level her off and get the airspeed built up. The end of the field was looming closer and closer. Again I brought the wheel back and the ground fell swiftly away as we clawed for altitude. At four hundred feet I leveled off, made my left turn and stole a sidelong glance at Bob. He had his face in his hands and was muttering into his palms. I eased the throttle back to what I hoped was cruising speed, and I saw Bob, out of the corner of my eye, shaking his head from side to side. He looked as though he were going to cry.

When I finally got to the downwind position to close

the throttle and make my one-eighty to land, I pulled
on the carb heat.

"How high are you?" asked Bob, with a look of revulsion on his face.

"Eight hundred feet," I answered cautiously.

"Look!" he said, tearing the wrapping-paper shield
from the altimeter. The needle indicated that we were
a mere four hundred feet above the ground.

As I eased down on my final approach, the stall-warning indicator set up a quick series of "beeeeps" which
told me I was near the edge of the stall, so I let the nose
drop a bit and crossed the fence with the controls firm
in my hand.

It took me twenty-six hundred feet of paved runway
to stop, brakes and all, so I knew I must have come in
awfully "hot."

As I turned around and taxied slowly back to take off,
I kept wishing that Bob would break down and give
me hell, but instead he sat there morosely, with the expression of a man who has just been stabbed in the back
by a friend. "Et tu, Frankus," his expression seemed to
say.

I looked around the sky for other planes in the pattern, headed her into the wind, and opened the throttle.

"Put your hands in your lap and keep them there,"
his voice snarled in my right ear. As I did, I looked at
him, and there sat Bob, with his arms folded. Both arms.
I reached out for the wheel which had moved out from
the panel as we began to roll. "Don't touch it!" he
shouted.

I sat there thinking, "This is the end. He's so mad
at me that he is going to kill us both!"

Then, suddenly, the little Cessna stopped bumping and took off at a beautiful rate of climb straight ahead, all by herself. Look, Ma, no hands!

After a few seconds, Bob's elbow caught me in the ribs. "Take a look around—*this* is four hundred feet! Now turn!" I turned ninety degrees to the left and reached for the throttle knob. Bob's hand closed over mine and the roar of the engine dropped appreciably.

"Listen to that sound," he said, nodding at the C-85 in front of us after he had retarded the throttle. . . . "Got it?" I numbly shook my head, yes. "Then *you* find it," he said, opening the throttle all the way.

I eased it back to what I thought was the right sound. "Again," he said, as the engine roared wide open under his touch. I hit the note again. "Now, find it," he said, closing the throttle all the way. I slid the knob forward and he nodded in approval.

Just as I began to feel better, my mood was shattered. "Well, are you going to land it or are you just going to clown around up here all day?" he asked sneeringly.

I came back to life and looked around. For the first time I realized that we were on our downwind leg at eight hundred feet.

I cut the throttle and made my turn onto base leg feeling the wheel go heavy in my hand. I ran the trim tab by my right knee back just enough to take the "pull" out of the wheel. The controls were getting softer now. Another left turn, and there was the runway out in front of me. As the edge of the field whipped past under us, I felt for the first time a sensation that can only be described as a "sigh" of the airplane, and the 140 landed so lightly that I didn't feel it hit, and rolled about three hundred feet.

Four times I went around the pattern without seeing an instrument, and on each landing I got the "sigh" as we landed, like the expiration of breath you experience when a trapeze artist almost falls, but doesn't.

As we rolled out from the last landing, I noticed that Bob was pulling the Scotch tape and wrapping paper off the panel. He was grinning, and I felt good.

"Next time I'll show him," I thought, as I taxied over towards the parking space.

"Stop," said Bob suddenly. I stepped on the toe brakes and looked around to see what we were about to run into. The right door popped open and Bob stepped out.

"Shoot a few by yourself and see how it feels," he said matter-of-factly, slammed the door, and walked away with his hands in his pockets.

In sort of a daze, I went to the end of the runway, ran through the usual procedure, and took off. My first solo was strictly routine. I can't even say that I was affected by the empty seat beside me, because even though Bob was not there himself, his voice was. I came in, felt the "sigh," and landed. My second and third landings were not nearly as good as the first one, but the "sigh" was there on each one. After three landings I called it a day and headed for the line, where I left the 140 tied down in the parking space. Bob was nowhere to be seen and I thought that I must have been pretty lousy if Bob left the field in disgust.

As I walked past the lunch room dejectedly, Bob called me and I went in. On the counter was a cup of hot coffee and a lighted cigarette, all ready for me, both of which hit the spot. I felt blue and disheartened, even though a solo was supposed to be a big thrill.

"Gosh, I'm tired," I said. "Even the plane seemed tired today—she sighed every time we got back to earth."

Bob grinned at me as I hunched over the cup of coffee and the cigarette.

"Dad, that's the feel of an airplane landing—what the old timers called 'seat of the pants flying.' When you can feel the stall, you are a flier."

As he fumbled around in his pockets looking for something, my mind raced backwards over my flight training under Angeli, and how it had affected me.

Little by little, the fear of the unknown and misunderstood had been painlessly removed from my subconscious—all of those obscure fears planted there throughout my life by ignorance, misstatement of fact and the jabbering of nervous "old women" of both sexes. Getting rid of this fear is the hardest part of the course of flight instruction; the course is designed to create confidence in the student—confidence that the engine will run and keep running; that the airplane will fly beautifully, mile after mile; that it will take off, even, with no hands on the controls; that an unusual attitude in the air is not unnatural, and can be controlled.

Little by little, as the engine clock ticked off the minutes I spent in the air, I developed that nebulous thing called the "feel" of flying, like the child who learns to ride his first bicycle. His father runs alongside holding him up, correcting his mistakes for hours; then suddenly, as if by magic, he rides—alone and unsupported. The first time he goes ten feet. The second time, ten yards. Then he has it, and never again will he have any trouble. For the rest of his life, he will have the "feel" of riding a bike.

And that's what the student pilot has to develop. Sometimes it comes quickly. Sometimes it takes a long time. Mysteriously enough, it seems that there is never any indication of when it is going to appear, until, like a flash of inspiration, one has it—the "feel" of flying.

Bob finally found what he was looking for in his pocket and handed me a little yellow piece of paper, my student license. On the back of it was written, "Qualified to solo Cessna 140." I had eight hours and twenty minutes of dual instruction on the log.

4. Navigation Is Spinach

I found that although I had my "solo ticket" I was by no means through with training, because the FAA required another thirty-two hours of flying instruction before I could get my pilot's license. Nine hours of this time had to be dual instruction and twenty-three supervised solo, including one solo cross-country flight of at least 100 miles with two landings on the way.

Being able to get an airplane up into the air and back on the ground again in one piece is the most fundamental aspect of the art of flying, but learning only that much does not make a pilot any more than being able to hit golf balls at a driving range makes one a golfer. Since the primary function of an airplane is safe, fast, economical transportation, the next part of the required course was concerned with the technique of cross-country flying, with heavy emphasis on navigation.

Bob taught me two types of navigation: "technical," as the FAA examiners require it, and "practical," as experienced pilots use it.

I can still remember a picture in my seventh-grade geography book of an old man with a long white beard, wearing a pointed hat and a robe inscribed with cabalistic designs. He was holding a telescope and staring wild-eyed at the heavens. It was titled simply, "The Navigator."

There are many things that have since escaped my memory, such as wedding anniversaries, where I parked the car, and, on occasion, the names of my various children; but any time I hear or read about navigation, up springs the image of the old guy with the beard.

No doubt the artist who produced that little gem accurately reflected the attitude of his time towards navigators, and it is highly understandable. For before I began to fly, I, like many people, regarded navigation as something mysterious, magical or even mystic. When a layman who might be inclined to drift into flying as a hobby runs head-on into a too-rich diet of such terms as "VOR," "correction angles," "computer ratios," "cross-fixes," "vector triangles," and the like, it is understandable that he might quickly retire from his ideas of flying, hie himself to the nearest sporting goods store and put down a payment on a set of matched clubs. I am sure that this fear of navigation keeps many people out of flying, yet it is completely unfounded. My thirteen-year-old son now navigates regularly for me, using Angeli's system, and he is no "A" student, either. Bob made it seem awfully easy.

Navigation, simply stated, is the technique of finding one's way from point A to point B. A and B may be two feet apart, or two thousand miles. When you go across the living room in the evening to turn on the television set, you are navigating on a small scale. You get out of your chair, A; look at the TV set, B; and proceed toward it. You go from A to B. In this problem you can see both

A and B, and other reference points around them: the coffee table on the left, the standing floor lamp behind it, the low chair on the right and, just beyond that, the TV set.

Now, suppose you are in bed late at night, and your wife, or mother, or someone else who can order you around, says, "Dear, I think I left the TV set turned on in the living room—go down and see." You stumble down the stairs, go into the darkened room, see the dim shadow of the coffee table on the left, the dark vertical shadow of the floor lamp behind it, then, in a few steps, you see the form of the low chair, then you feel out behind that for the TV set, which was undoubtedly turned off in the first place.

These two examples, in a greatly simplified way, entail as much navigation as private pilots must perform in the usual cross-country flight.

There are in our illustrations two basic forms of navigation: "pilotage," which is navigation by visual landmarks, from one point of reference to another, and "dead reckoning," which is used when the points of reference are quite a bit farther apart or are for one reason or another invisible.

In pilotage aloft you do exactly the same thing that you do crossing the living room, only, instead of coffee tables, lamps and chairs, you use cities, rivers, mountains, highways or railroads, as shown on the aeronautical charts.

Most earthlings (this is a word that I picked up from a science-fiction book, and I apologize for it—but what other word *is* there to describe nonfliers?) have the idea that the air is as clear as a bottle of gin; that once you have climbed up a thousand feet you see all the way to the horizon.

Unfortunately, this condition of unlimited visibility is very rare. Usually the atmosphere contains a certain amount of moisture which is more dense close to the surface of the earth and is called "ground haze." Around cities this ground haze is reinforced by smoke which is called "smog" or "smaze," and it is a good day when the visibility is more than twelve miles—and that sure isn't the horizon!

It is unusual in the East to have the weatherman tell you "visibility twenty to twenty-five miles," and I have been up on relatively few "CAVU"—"ceiling and visibility unlimited"—days. But on such a day, when the air is free of smoke, haze or smog, you can see to the horizon; from three thousand feet the horizon is eighty miles away; from eight thousand feet it is almost a hundred and twenty miles. From that easy chair in the sky you can see the curvature of the earth and you will never again have any doubts that Columbus was right. Gill Robb Wilson called it "The Airman's World," and it is a thrilling view when you see clear to the edge.

Suppose you intend to fly from Atlantic City to Wings Field just north of Philadelphia, and the "rainmaker" has told you that visibility will be no better than twelve miles all the way.

You lay out your chart and draw a straight line from Bader Field, Atlantic City, to Wings, marking the line off roughly in segments of twenty-five miles (thirteen minutes apart at a hundred and ten mph). Then you note on the chart that twelve miles (six and a half minutes) from Bader there is a large military airport directly on course (the coffee table). Alongside that runs a railroad track, paralleled by a concrete highway (the floor lamp). In another ten to twelve minutes there is a town with a clearly marked Airport (the low chair); then just beyond that is the City of Philadelphia. From there, finding Wings is simple, because there are a lot of landmarks close together.

That is pilotage. Easy?

When you don't have many easily recognizable features in view at all times along the way, either because there are none—such as over large bodies of water, or mountains or plains—or because the visibility is down to three miles, so that you can't see well enough to go by pilotage, you go by dead reckoning.

Dead reckoning is a phrase that used to frighten me. It sounded so final. The old "navigator" had swapped his telescope for a lily.

Actually the word "dead" is a peculiar contraction of the word "deduced," and navigation by dead reckoning consists of calculating by simple arithmetic how far you will go on a certain course in a certain time at a certain speed.

Suppose you leave position A, headed north to position B, one hundred miles away. The plane cruises at a hundred mph, so you take off, circle to gain altitude, head north, set the clock and fly by compass. In an hour, with no wind blowing at all, you deduce that you should be at B. All you need is a chart, a ruler, a compass and a clock.

This simple solution is subject, however, to endless variations: a tail wind will get you there faster; a head wind will hold you back. A wind from the side will blow you off the course, unless you compensate for it. And then there is the light-plane compass, which is as skittish as a cat at a dog show, and not quite as predictable.

If the nose goes up, the magnetic compass spins one way; if it goes down, it spins another. If you are flying North and turn East or West, the compass needle lags behind and, if you make a turn when flying South, the compass races into the turn much faster than the plane. Then, there are iron deposits in the ground which cause the needle to point in the craziest directions, and you see notes on the chart like this: "WARNING: Magnetic variation in vicinity of Wilmington at ground elevation differs from normal as much as 4 to 14 degrees." The only thing to do is fly as straight as you can for fifteen seconds, give the needle a chance to settle down, and then sneak a quick look at it to have an approximate idea of your heading.

Furthermore, the compass doesn't really point to the magnetic pole in about 80 per cent of the airplanes I have flown because every time some new piece of metal is added to the panel—such as a new radio, a gyro compass or a clock—the compass is affected, and this can really complicate a navigation problem.

I remember one flight particularly well. It all started with my having to take some corporation papers to Atlantic City to be signed at a board meeting. Tom called me at about eleven-thirty at the office and told me he had rented a Piper Super-Cub and asked if I wanted a ride to the seashore. Naturally, I said yes and flagged a cab to Camden Airport, where Tom was waiting for me on the apron.

It was a miserable day. Drizzle came down intermittently from the leaden sky. "Weather" told us that the cloud base drifting slowly overhead was only twenty-five hundred feet high, but assured us that it would hold for two or three hours—long enough to get to the shore and back, which was about forty minutes each way.

The Super-Cub is a tandem job in which the pilot and passenger sit one behind the other. I got in the back seat with my documents, while Tom acted as throttle bender up front in the "office."

As he climbed the Super-Cub out at Camden Airport, I leaned forward and spoke in his ear.

"Tom, follow that double-track railroad southeast; it goes right into Bader Field on a direct line." He curled his lip at me over his shoulder.

"I'm a navigator, not a railroad engineer—I'll follow the compass."

"*That* for me," I thought. "Well, he's the pilot, so let him do it his way." As we circled the field to get altitude, I glanced at my watch. It was one-thirty.

I got out my brief case and began to leaf through the blue-backed documents that I had to present to the company officers and became immersed in corporation jargon.

After what seemed to be a few minutes, I looked up to see where we were. The clouds were breaking up a little, but we still couldn't see the sun, and the land below didn't look familiar at all. We should have been in sight of a straight-as-a-ruler double railroad track and a six-lane highway paralleling it, but there was nothing in sight but scrub pines for six miles on either side.

I leaned forward and touched Tom on the shoulder. "Where are we?" I asked.

"Almost there," he answered confidently, but I looked at my watch and saw the time: 2 P.M. We should have seen the ocean by now. Two-fifteen went past, then two-thirty. I saw beads of sweat on the back of Tom's neck. Make fun of us railroad pilots would he—this will teach him!

Finally he pointed to an acute angle of concrete runways below to our right.

"Here's where we are," he said. "Millville Airport."

"Millville, my eye," I answered. "You better land and find where we are, or we're out a client."

That struck home; he tilted her over in a spiral turn and greased her on the smooth runway. Imagine our chagrin, shock, consternation and disgust when we learned from the sign on the front of the hangar, that we had landed, not at Millville Airport, which is in South Jersey, but less than twenty miles from Trenton. The airport we had seen from on high was McGuire Air Force Base. We were about eighty miles away from Atlantic City, more than seventy degrees off course, led astray by slavish attention to an errant compass.

We took off immediately and for the next forty minutes we struggled through lowering clouds with the help of Gulf Oil Company road maps, finally reaching the Garden State Parkway which stands out from the air like a ribbon on a rug.

"I'll make a concrete compass navigator out of you yet," I growled into his ear as we rode the parkway almost into Bader Field two hours late. He didn't say a word, which is unusual.

We found out later that someone had put the compass out of balance by removing some radio gear, but had not mentioned it to anyone; whenever a change is made in the metallic mass of a plane, it is necessary to go through a rigmarole to see how far off the magnetic compass is as the result of such change, to notify the pilot of the amount of deviation so that he can allow for it in navigating by dead reckoning.

The plane is taken to some part of the field where a large circle representing a magnetic compass rose is painted on the ground and the plane is pointed towards the magnetic north. The compass may read 003 degrees. This is repeated to the east, south and west. When you get through, there is a little card hung over the compass: "For north steer 003 degrees," et cetera.

Furthermore, the magnetic pole to which the compass points is not located at the true pole, but is situated somewhere in Canada, so you must allow for this factor, too. It is called "magnetic variation" and in my part of the country varies around eight to ten degrees "west variation." On the West Coast it is an easterly variation.

In ground school they give you a formula to help make solving navigation problems "easy."

First you draw a line from A to B on the chart. Then you measure the direction represented by an angle computed from "true" north, and write that down. Then you add (or subtract) the amount of the "magnetic variation" to the actual direction of "magnetic" north for your part of the world; the result gives you your "magnetic course." But don't forget the compass deviation factor from the little card, which must be added (or subtracted) to get your "compass course," or the number you steer by.

Thus, your formula is: $T \pm V = M \pm D = C$, which means "true course, plus or minus variation, equals magnetic course, plus or minus deviation, equals compass course."

And how do you remember these magic initials? With catch phrases: "True Virgins Make Dull Company,"

"The Vagrant Moved Down California," or in reverse: "Can Ducks Make Vertical Turns?" "Can Dead Men Vote Twice?" Ain't it awful?

We haven't yet figured the effect of wind on our course through the blue. This is officially covered by the study of wind vectors and wind correction angles—but, believe me, we aren't going to get into them in this book! There is an easier way; and I hope when you learn it you will understand why I say, to paraphrase the *New Yorker* cartoon, that "Navigation is spinach, and to hell with it."

In our dual cross-country flights, Bob soon taught me that navigation for private pilots is just as easy as hiking through the woods with a compass. With no gobbledegook, Bob taught me his system, which we called "Kentucky windage."

Let's take a realistic look at the average "week-end pilot"—the man flies for recreation and maybe occasionally for business. He flies during daylight hours and when the surface visibility is pretty good, about five or six miles at the least. The airplane he flies usually cruises at less than a hundred and thirty mph airspeed. For him, eight thousand feet is *high,* and his typical cross-country flight is less than two hundred miles each way.

His situation is no different from that of a Boy Scout hiking through the woods, who sets a compass course, sights to a tree ahead of him on the course line, walks to that tree, then takes another sighting on his compass to another tree and then walks to that tree, until, many trees later, he arrives at his destination. The difference is that the boy in the woods has a tougher job, because, if he misses his destination by a hundred yards, he may be lost; whereas a pilot can be six or seven miles off course, and still see his check point.

My partner and I represent the two completely opposite approaches to the subject. He admits he would rather navigate than fly. I have often suspected that he flies just so he can navigate. We have made cross-country trips together in my Cessna 140 on which I am sure he hasn't seen anything but the chart in his lap, the stop watch hanging from the cord around his neck, and the check points below. He plans his flights to the minute before he takes off, marking numerous check points along the way, and noting the precise time he should hit each one. If he gets a little off to one side of the course line, he whips out an Air Force E6B computer and sets up an off-course problem, just for fun.

Lest any prospective flier be frightened by the word "computer," let's explain that right now. A computer is merely a rotating series of scales which, when adjusted, set up problems and answers with a flick of the thumb, so that you don't have to compute with pencil and paper. Two scales are all that I use, although there are many additional computations that can and must be done on the E6B by instrument pilots. The A scale sets either to "Miles" or "Gallons." The B scale sets up "time in minutes." Thus, if you cruise 100 mph, you put the 100 on the A scale, next to the 60 (minutes) on the B scale, and, if you look at the 25 on the A, you will see that it lines up with the 15 on the B. In other words, in 15 minutes (with no wind) you will have traveled 25 miles. Likewise, if you know that your engine burns five gallons of gas per hour, you match 5 A with 60 B; then 120 B (two hours) would be opposite 10 A. In two hours you will burn 10 gallons. It's that easy. So let's forget all the other functions of the computer, and remember only the A and B scales.

Not long ago Tom and I flew from Wings Field to Lock Haven eighty-five miles northwest of Harrisburg —to look at the new Piper Comanche. As usual, we flipped a coin to see who should fly the outbound leg, and he won.

The New York sectional chart was soon spread on the stabilizer, and the flight was planned about the same way an engineer builds a bridge. First, he laid out a "rhumb line," which is only the technical name for the straight line from the point of departure to the point of destination. From then on he threw figures around like an accountant during income tax season. He consulted notes on winds aloft from the Weather Bureau, measured angles and distances, used every scale on the E6B computer, front *and* back, and frequently flashed into action with a small pencil sharpener. While I stood around courting a stroke, he invoked the old question, "Can Ducks Make Vertical Turns," and ran off a column of figures. He drew vector diagrams, showing wind correction angles to get a "true heading." He put down ETA's (estimated time of arrival) to every check point, then got a pressure altitude figure, then computed "true airspeed," and I don't know what else.

By the time we took off, my clothes were out of style, but we were flight-planned like a SAC bomber.

In about half an hour we were purring along at a hundred and ten mph, 3500 feet over the foothills of the Alleghenies, with my buddy on the wheel, throttle, chart, computer, straightedge, protractor, stop watch and timetable—and with me smoking a cigarette, idly gazing at the scenery and listening to dance music on the headphones.

Suddenly we hit turbulence over the mountains and the 140 began to bounce around like a cork in the surf. The magnetic compass spun violently from side to side as the plane kicked around and ye pilot gave his entire undivided attention just to keeping her upright. His pencil was clenched in his teeth, the stop watch swung pendulum-like from the string around his neck, the chart slipped unnoticed to the floor, and the computer was thrown back on the shelf. For ten minutes we flew thus, then finally slid into smoother air. By the time the dust settled and we retrieved the charts, we were lost. The last check point was about twenty miles behind, and neither of us knew what the next one was, let alone where it was.

I took over while he peered around, searching for something—anything—that looked familiar. Finally, he "estimated" that we were ten miles south of our course, saying that the wind must have switched ninety degrees on us. While I continued to fly the 140, he went through the entire procedure of correcting for the lost course, which meant that he started from scratch and laid out a brand new rhumb line, new check points, new headings, all based on his *estimate* of the wind direction and velocity. This is no mean physical feat in a cramped cabin, working on a folded chart in your lap under a moving control wheel, while the airplane is rolling and pitching around the sky. I just hate to think of trying to do it up there by myself!

But that's just my point—it isn't necessary to do what he did at all.

In the first place, I'll be darned if anyone can hold a magnetic compass course within three to five degrees with the average light-plane compass. The "pros" use gyro compasses for this very reason.

In the second place, this stuff about ducks and vertical turns can get you into a lot of trouble on a long cross-country flight by heading you off in the wrong direction if you add annual variation when you should have subtracted it.

And why worry about the ducks and their vertical turns, anyhow? In the East, at least, it is a waste of time. Take a good look at a sectional chart. It is covered with circles on which are printed compass directions, the centers of the circles being Omni Radio ranges. On the back of the chart it is stated: "Bearings are magnetic *at the station.*" In other words, any line parallel to the course line and bisecting an Omni station compass rose will show the correct compass heading for that part of the course. Your variation is already figured out for you by the cartographers.

In the third place, unless you are certain of wind direction and velocity, the entire problem is pure hokum in the first place.

So what is this navigating technique that I claim is so great? Simply point-to-point pilotage, à la Boy Scout, plus what the old-fashioned riflemen used to call "Kentucky windage." Those old-timers didn't have our modern adjustable sights; they simply sighted in their rifles on calm days, and, when there was a breeze, they aimed to the windward side of the target or "held off" to put the bullet into the bull's-eye.

On our dual cross-country flights in the rag-wing Cessna, we used this technique: first, we would lay our course line broken into hundred-mile segments, with prominent check points marked about every twenty-five miles, or every fifteen minutes of flying. Then, we would note the compass headings given on the map, using the compass roses of the Omni stations. Then, having filed a flight plan by telephone, we would take off and get on course as soon as possible, watching the compass and the clock from time to time.

Within ten to fifteen minutes we would have covered twenty to twenty-five miles and the first check point would be somewhere in sight. Suppose we were off course five degrees to the left—the check point was only three miles over to the right, which isn't much from the air. Did we then haul out a computer and set up an off-course problem? Heck, no! We would line up the compass, sight ahead to some prominent point of the terrain four or five minutes away—the equivalent to the Boy Scout's "next tree"—and fly to it, "holding off" a mite to the right, or into the wind. In fifteen minutes we would see check point number two, as marked on the chart. If we overdid this "holding off," we might find the second check point to our left. Usually it came up in the arc of the propeller.

In clear weather this works like a charm, with no bookkeeping at all, and you can spend your time looking at the scenery, watching for other air traffic, and just plain relaxing.

No "Ducks." No "Dead Men." Kentucky windage. Try it sometime. Works swell!

5. Needle Work

It was only after I had learned to navigate cross country pretty well by pilotage and dead reckoning that Bob allowed me to use the radio receivers in the 140 for anything other than listening to dance music and news broadcasts. He used to say, "You have to creep before you can walk."

In the first few weeks of flying I had accumulated a huge pile of Sectional Charts from the Coast and Geodetic Survey, covering the United States from border to border, and every night before nodding off to dreamland I flew my bed on wings of imagination to all corners of the country.

I have been fascinated by all kinds of maps and charts ever since I was old enough to know which way north was, and it didn't take me long to see that the government's aeronautical charts were by far the most informative I had ever glommed; they showed rivers, lakes, reservoirs, towns, features of the terrain, towers, dams, bridges, railroad tracks, highways, power and pipe lines, exactly as they appeared from the air.

Sectional charts have to be good and accurate because they are designed to be used by contact pilots. Thus all possible visual checkpoints must be faithfully reproduced. But they also seemed to be cluttered with a lot of things I couldn't comprehend: four-inch circles, which resembled what in the Navy we used to call compass roses, and blue lines interconnecting these circles, and little blue boxes with numbers, some printed in red, some in blue. Some of the rectangles on the charts contained the word "radio," and around the edges were references to radio frequencies, which I didn't understand, and I began to wonder whether I needed a code book to make sense of all these jottings.

"What is this radio range stuff all about—and is it English?" I asked Bob one day as we walked out to the Cessna for a check ride.

He gave me a funny look for a moment, then started to untie the wing ropes.

"O.K., Dad," he smiled as he tossed the right wing rope to the ground and removed the chocks from the right landing wheel, "I guess you are ready to learn some more about the art of airplane driving."

He took a deep breath, folded his arms across his chest, and toed the ground.

"There are various kinds of radio navigation aids, beginning with the low frequency range, the old four-leg system that was established back in the middle nineteen-thirties. More than any other single development, radio navigation aids have been responsible for making all-weather flight scheduling possible for the airlines. The old four-leg ranges were known as 'aural ranges,' which means in plain English that you had to determine your position and course and instrument approach procedures by what you heard over a low frequency radio receiver; you literally had to depend upon your ears to ride a 'beam.' One of the major problems with that was that if there were any thunderstorms around—when you really *needed* to hear the signal—it was broken up by the crashing static associated with lightning discharges."

He began to untie the ropes from the left wing while I followed him around like an executive.

"That system was improved—oh, about nineteen-forty— by the type of radio operating in the very high frequency spectrum, which is abbreviated in print as 'VHF'; during World War II a few radio ranges of the four-leg ranges were established using VHF so that the aural beam could be heard clearly without static interference. Those were called 'very high frequency aural ranges' or 'VARs.'

"Then, a few years later, the military developed another system which transmitted, not just four legs, but a leg for every one of the three hundred and sixty degrees in a circle, also on VHF; these are the principal navigation aids we have now, and they are called 'VORs,' which stands for 'very high frequency omnidirectional radio ranges.' Best of all, they designed a receiver for aircraft that enables the pilot to isolate and select any one of the so-called 'radials' from the VORs and have a display on the panel to show him accurately where he is with respect to it by a deflecting needle."

He shook his head slightly as if in annoyance as he kicked the chocks away from the left wheel.

"I'm making it sound hard. Look here on the chart."

We spread the Washington Sectional on the grass and knelt over it to examine it closely; I guess we looked like a couple of crap shooters.

"Remember this, first of all," cautioned Bob, shaking his finger under my nose, "any time you see a red marking of any sort on a chart, especially a red number, it refers to a low frequency radio facility, which you can receive only on low frequency equipment, like a radio direction finder. Any time you see a blue mark, line or number, it refers to a VHF radio facility. In either case, the number is the frequency of the facility that you tune in and listen to. If you just remember that much, you shouldn't have any trouble with radio work.

"You have two types of radio receivers in the plane: low frequency and VHF, and never the twain shall meet; the low frequency receiver will not receive VHF, or vice versa."

He stubbed his index finger at the chart before us.

"Notice how these VOR, or 'omni,' ranges are related. Most of them are situated within fifty miles of each other so that you can ride a continuous radio signal on regularly defined highways of the sky, called Federal Airways, to any place in the country. These airways are called 'Victor Airways' and are numbered, with the odd numbers running north and south and the even numbers running east and west. All you have to do is select a Victor Airway, tune in to the omni ranges along the route, set the VOR receiver and omni bearing selector to pick out the inbound or outbound radial you want, keep the needle centered in the VOR indicator, and go on your way. When you fly along airways under visual flight rules, be especially careful to keep at the proper altitudes: any direction between 001° and 180° you are at an odd altitude plus 500 feet; between 181° and 360°, an even altitude plus 500 feet, i.e.: 4500 feet, 6500 feet . . .

"Suppose you want to fly to Miami in your little bird,

you would start the trip on a westerly heading at 4500 feet, say, but when you turn the corner down by Jacksonville, you will have to go down to 3500 or up to 5500 feet. Since the people on Instrument Flight Plans fly on assigned 'hard' altitudes or at the even thousands, such as 4000, 5000, 6000, and so forth, you are separated from them by aviation's rules of the road; since everyone going the same direction is flying at the same altitude, it prevents those high rate of closure, head-on situations."

He pointed out that Victor 3 would probably be my aerial route. "See how the radial from Modena VOR goes to Westminster VOR and takes you past Washington, right on down to Raleigh-Durham? That's how you would get all the way to Miami. Get it?"

I thought I did. I could smell orange blossoms.

"Come on, Ace," he said, scrambling to his feet. "Let's try it once."

As we trundled out to the end of the runway, Bob folded the Washington Sectional to show the Atlantic City area and said, "I've told you all you need to know to find Atlantic City airport by using your radio equipment. Now, go ahead and find it."

I took off, heading in a generally southeasterly direction to three thousand feet, just above a pretty dense ground haze. When I finally trimmed her out for cruise, I began to study the chart.

"Atlantic City . . . Where the heck is it? . . . Oh, there it is, and there is the compass rose close to the beach and there is the blue VOR frequency. Now what?

"How do I tune it in?" I asked as a DC-3 slid by under us on a final approach to the North Philadelphia Airport.

"Look at the box next to the omni rose which is centered on the VOR station; that is the frequency to tune the VOR receiver in on."

Sure enough, adjacent to the omni rose was a little blue box that said, "Atlantic City ACY/·— —·—· —·— —/ 108.6." I tuned the omni receiver to 108.6 megacycles (they call them megaHertz now) and heard the identifier: dit dah, dah dit dah dit, dah dit dah dah and recognized the Morse code for ACY. That was it! I looked at Bob with a surprised expression that meant, "Look what I found," and he just smiled.

I rotated the omni bearing knob until the needle centered and I saw the number at the bottom of the dial: 158.

I turned to a heading of 158° on the compass and flew so as to keep the needle centered—if it edged off to the right, I turned slightly to the right until it centered again. In twenty minutes the big airport appeared ahead of us in the slight haze as if by magic.

"Good show, Dad," said Bob. "Now you know how to find an omni station by navigation radio."

Just then a voice broke in over the identifier which had been beeping away all the time: "Weather forecast. Atlantic City: ceiling, ten thousand feet, scattered clouds at five thousand; visibility four to five miles in haze; temperature 78, dew point 68; New York . . ." Bob reached over and snapped off the radio switch and I slid the right headphone up on the side of my head above my ear.

"The radio stations on the ground, called Flight Service stations, give local and area weather on a regular basis, using the VOR frequency," he said, handing me a lighted cigarette and punching the lighter in again for his own. "When you are flying cross country, you can get weather information ahead any time by calling in to the Flight

Service stations along the route. You call them on 121.1 and listen to the VOR frequency to get updated informa- tion so that on a long cross-country flight you can always know what is happening up the line. A pilot who runs into bad weather has no one to blame but himself."

"This radio is really terrific," I said, trying to figure my course to get home. "But whatever happened to those old low frequency radio beams? And why should I have a low frequency receiver if there are none any more?"

Bob smiled. I wasn't sure whether it was at my naïveté in asking such a question or my obvious plight of not know- ing how to get back to Wings.

"This is really quite simple," he said, turning the nav radio on again. "You will remember how you flew toward Atlantic City with the omni bearing needle indicating 'To,' and that all you had to do was keep the needle cen- tered by flying toward the direction it pointed to keep on the electronic track. If you imagine that there is a wire stretching from the VOR station and that your omni needle is pointing to it, like an underground trolley pole reaches toward the underground wire, you can envision how the system works to keep you on the proper track over the ground."

Bob broke out the Sectional Chart again as he talked.

"Now, if you want to get back to Wings, what you do is lay out a line on the chart from the Atlantic City VOR directly to Wings, in this case it is about 330°, as you can see the line I have just marked crosses the rim of the omni rose on Atlantic City. Watch what I do: I have the omni set tuned into ACY—hear the identifier? Always listen for the identifier so you will be sure that you have not tuned into the wrong VOR, which can happen if they change frequencies—then rotate the omni bearing selector to 330. Now you will see that the omni needle is all the way to the right side of the dial and that the indicator reads 'From.' That shows that the outbound radial from Atlantic City to Wings is to the right of your position, so if you fly 330° you will run parallel to it, more or less, depending on the wind."

He drew a line toward the track line he had already laid out.

"Whatcha do is fly in intercept at about 30° toward the course, in this case due North," he said, turning the wheel and pointing the spinner toward New York. "Now watch that needle."

In a couple of minutes the needle edged off the extreme right side of the dial and Bob told me to slowly start to turn toward the 330° track. When the needle finally centered, he snapped his fingers. "On course," he said. "Now keep it there."

In a few minutes the familiar terrain around Wings Field appeared, and I knew that I was back where I started, entirely by following radio signals via a needle on the instrument panel. I didn't have to listen to anything—except the identifier—and in practice it was a lot easier than when I had tried to learn how to do it out of a book. It is so much easier when you actually *do* it in an airplane.

For the next few days I flew solo to all sorts of places: Harrisburg, Wilkes-Barre, Elmira, Poughkeepsie, just to learn how to use Omni facilities, until I finally knew how to locate myself with a high degree of accuracy in a few minutes.

Don't ever believe anyone who says that he never gets

lost while flying; he is ribbing you. One time someone asked Daniel Boone whether he had ever been lost in the woods, to which Dan'l is said to have replied no, he had never been *lost,* but once he was bewildered for a few days. What he meant was that it took him that long to locate himself.

One time twenty-five hundred feet over the foggy Catskills en route to Philadelphia I became aware that the hills below looked perplexingly alike and nothing in sight resembled any of the details on the chart I held in my lap. Did I tremble? Did I sweat? No . . . , I tuned the Narco Omnigator in to Wilkes-Barre Omni, spun the radial selector until the needle centered, noted the radial (073), then did the same thing with Poughkeepsie Omni (282), then drew lines from those two compass roses on the chart. Where the two lines intersected was my position at that moment—Grossinger's resort. The whole operation took one minute and nine seconds—lost and found.

From time to time I noticed another type of radio facility on the charts: a transparent red circle maybe three quarters of an inch in diameter, with an adjacent box very similar to the Omni range station boxes, printed in red like this: "Selinsgrove Radio 353 SEG · · · · – – · ."

"What is this?" I asked Bob the next time I saw him, indicating the circle at Selinsgrove.

"Did you ever tune it in?" he asked twinkling his eyes at me.

"Yes," I answered, "but all I can get is the call letters over and over again, and what good is that?"

"Those symbols on the chart show the location of non-directional radio beacons, and they are spread all over the chart. See, here's one at Atlantic City and here's one at Binghamton . . ."

"Nondirectional, that's a new one to me," I said. "How can I use them?"

"You can't, because you don't have the equipment for it, but come here and I'll show you how it works."

We stepped up on the wing of a Bonanza parked on the line and got into the cabin. When I had arranged myself comfortably he pointed to a rectangular black radio on the panel mounted just below an Omni set.

"This is a low-frequency radio which has a special circuit connected to this instrument"—he indicated a circular dial on the panel.

He snapped on the radio switch and pushed in the circuit-breaker-type master switch and in a moment I heard a hum from the speaker mounted in the ceiling. Bob switched to the broadcast band, twirled the station selector to 1060 kilocycles, and in a moment we heard a news broadcast from station WRCV whose transmitter is about a mile south of Wings. At the same moment the needle on the dial came to life and swung around to what would be three o'clock on a timepiece.

"That is the automatic direction finder showing us that WRCV is to the right of the airplane. Now if we were aloft and wanted to fly to Selinsgrove, or Atlantic City, or Binghamton, and we didn't have Omni equipment, we could tune in to the low-frequency signal of those beacons according to the frequency given on the chart (making sure that we were tuned to the right one by the call letters that it sends out every few seconds) .

"Suppose you tune in Selinsgrove and the ADF needle

points to the left (nine o'clock) , you turn the airplane left until the needle pointed straight up, which would indicate that the range was directly ahead of the plane. As long as the needle is pointed straight up you will fly like a homing pigeon and hit the station sooner or later. You can use either the FAA radio beacons, or the commercial broadcast stations for this. Any wonder that the old-time pilots call it the 'bird dog'?"

"Why didn't somebody tell me these things?" I asked throwing my hands up in the air. "Why make me fly from landmark to landmark when the visibility is down to two or three miles straining my eyes for a check point when these Omni and ADF sets give check points hundreds of miles wide?"

"Well, I'll tell you, Dad: fuses blow, and batteries split, and tubes burn out and short circuits develop—these radio sets are subjected to a terrific beating—and you have to know how to fly without radio because the most wonderful set in the world is nothing but a couple of bucks' worth of junk if one five-cent condenser burns out. Sure I want you to use radio. The Federal Aviation Administration spends a barrel of money for your safety when it sets up radio facilities, but radio is only an aid, and knowing its use is only a part of being a pilot. You still have to know dead reckoning and pilotage and you should still check your position visually on the chart; don't for heaven's sake get the idea that radio has made the old-fashioned flying by common sense obsolete."

I still look over the side once in a while when on a business trip to see where I am, but between you and me I do most of my navigating by means of those needles on the panel, no strain, no worry—just the way my wife knits at the movies. I don't even have to think about it any more. It has become automatic, reflexive, subconscious. Like knitting, navigation is a cinch after you have learned how to work the needles.

6. Blindman's Buff

On July first I made my first fairly long cross-country flight entirely on my own—seventy miles to Ocean City, New Jersey.

Every year, the day school lets out, my wife and three sons move bag and baggage to the Jersey shore, usually making me a summer bachelor because I can't take automobile traffic any more. But I determined that while building up time for my private pilot license I should commute by air between Philadelphia and the beach.

The night before my sortie I had studied the chart until I knew every mile of the course better than I know the back of my mother-in-law's hand, of which I have seen a great deal since I took up flying. Even after I turned off the night-table lamp at 2 A.M., I tossed around in bed until the first light of dawn.

After a day at the office—during which I tried to work in short bursts between telephone calls to the weather bureau and hikes to the window to squint at the sky—I drove out to Wings.

As I loosened the tie down ropes from the struts, the balmy breezes were caressing the long grass on the fields, and the sun was a brilliant fireball whose warm rays were periodically intercepted by the few fat fluffy white clouds marching slowly overhead like so many well-laundered sheep.

"What a day for my maiden voyage," I thought to myself as I tossed the ropes aside and watched an Aero Commander shoot a touch-and-go landing.

After giving the airplane a thorough preflight check as I had been instructed to do so many times, I kicked the chocks away from the wheels, climbed in, yelled "clear," and started the engine.

As I fastened my safety belt and waited for the oil pressure to register, I looked around feeling very much superior to everyone else in the world who was not the great flier I was.

My imagination raced ahead through time into the future history books of flight: the Wright Brothers, Lindbergh, Wiley Post, Frank Smith—pioneers. The oil pressure came up just when I was composing a few paragraphs to be placed under my name in "Who's Who." Oh, well, that could wait until I made a few world-shaking flights, to Ocean City, for instance, over the aboriginal wastes of New Jersey.

I opened the throttle and the engine roared as the plane moved ahead about three inches and—stopped! I opened the throttle farther, but the plane wouldn't budge. What with all the racket of the wide-open engine on the parking line and my sliding around on my seat looking out of the windows to see what was in front of the wheels, a small group of spectators soon gathered, pointing their fingers and laughing fit to kill themselves. One of the line crew came up, shouting between cupped hands, but I couldn't hear him because of the engine. I cut the switch, opened the door and angrily asked, "What the heck is wrong with this thing, anyhow?"

He leaned over to me, as if disclosing a state secret, and whispered in my ear: "You forgot to untie the tail wheel."

I sat glumly in the plane while the line boy untied the tail-wheel rope and then, to a round of applause, which I didn't particularly relish, I taxied to the end of the runway, checked out the mags and gave her the gun.

My confidence was not destroyed, merely shaken, by my dumb stunt of trying to taxi while still anchored to a concrete block embedded in the earth, but Bob told me that this is not uncommon to nervous new pilots; that's why it is good for a novice to use a printed check list every time he flies a plane, for the first few hours, anyway.

Despite the slight jangle, my nerves quickly settled down as we began to pound down the paved runway. The airspeed came up—30, 40, 45, 50—and I eased back on the wheel and we lifted graceful as a gull into the cool, clean air. As we broke ground I leaned over and set the altimeter at 330, rolled the gyro compass to 160, caged it, and then made my exit from the traffic pattern. The C-85 was running smooth as silk, the chart was in my lap, the rate of climb indicator showed an even 250 feet per minute, airspeed 90, and I had 1500 feet of air under me when the nerves got jangled again.

Maybe someday an engineer will explain to me how an inanimate machine like an airplane engine realizes that it is over a place where the pilot can't land. So long as the terrain below is flat farm land, or sandy beaches, or studded with golf courses, the engine purrs along like a big cat; but just let it find itself over the ocean, or in a mountain pass, or low over the heart of a city, and the engine takes on the frantic note of a concrete mixer loaded with bricks. Pilots refer to this as the engine going into "automatic rough," so everyone seems to have had the same experience at one time or another; but when it happens without warning, the gray hairs break out on your scalp like mushrooms after a summer rain.

There I was (as the boys in the Air Force are wont to say when relating their experiences) over the heart of North Philadelphia with its gridlike pattern of row houses, when suddenly the engine began to sound mighty uneven in its operation. My mind raced to consider the possibilities of mechanical failure: Loss of oil pressure? Pressure gauge says O. K. Bearing overheating? Temperature gauge seems O. K. Loose connecting rod? I didn't even know what a connecting rod was, but I had read about them somewhere and the word came back to scare me. What could it be? Where could I land if the darn thing did quit on me? I looked everywhere for a park, long road, or railroad yard, but there was nothing closer than Camden Airport, a long eight miles ahead. The engine began to sound worse, and yet all I could do was sit there and pray. My wife says that a watched pot never boils—the same thing was true about that C-85. By the clock, it took eleven minutes from take-off for me to be over the Delaware River Bridge, but it seemed like eleven hours. I kept hitting the clock on the panel and shaking my wrist watch, both of which had apparently stopped in sympathy with the engine's difficulties; then, as soon as I saw Camden Airport, the roughness up front smoothed out into a steady drone of power. The engine knew! So did the clocks, which again began to keep perfect time.

After taking several deep breaths to get my heart back to normal, and laughing at myself for being so upset, I sat back to relax. I opened the window to let the cool air swirl around in the little cabin, and put my left elbow on the ledge, as I often do when driving a car. The slip stream went up my rolled-up sleeve, and billowed my shirt out like a parachute. That's one way to dry a shirt!

Going a hundred and ten mph, I looked down from the open window at thousands and thousands of automobiles rolling slowly, bumper to bumper, towards the seashore points, getting away from the heat of the city. They looked like lines of paint-speckled ants, crawling across the bridges, around traffic circles, along the highways, as far as the eye could see. Below me were four lines of cars inching around Camden Airport Circle, starting and stopping in a series of undulating movements like a wooly worm taking a stroll in the springtime. I knew from personal experience that the drivers were hot, tired and churning inside. They honked their horns, glared at one another and muttered oaths in their irritation. Some of them, sooner or later, would become so frustrated that they would lose their reason and take terrible chances, speeding, and cutting in and out, with no regard for anyone's safety.

I remembered how frazzled I used to be when I finally did get to the seashore; how I snapped at the children and growled at my poor wife. "Keep away from Daddy for an hour" was the motto. But that admonition was a thing of the past. I reached back into the luggage compartment, where my suit coat hung on a wire coat hanger, and fished out a cigarette. As I lighted it, I turned on the radio to B.C. and put the big surplus Navy headphones over my ears. In a moment I was listening to recorded dance music—cool, relaxed and supremely happy.

Looking down past my left landing wheel, hanging motionless five feet below my window, I watched the flat South Jersey real estate unreel: towns, farms, apartment houses, race tracks, factories and miles and miles of scrub pine.

I was truly entranced at the sight. For thirty-five years I had gone from Philadelphia to Ocean City by auto and by train, yet I suddenly realized that I had never really seen Jersey before. The little towns, hidden back in the woods, the roads, fire breaks, power lines and lakes, thousands of lakes, which I never realized existed, and railroad tracks in all directions. I followed tracks along with my eye trying to locate them on the chart.

Off to my left, I saw a complicated railroad intersection with tracks curving and joining, and my previous night's study dropped the junction into its proper location on my course. "Winslow Junction," near Hammonton, my halfway point, and it was just twenty minutes since I had taken off from Wings. I thought of the people who were on the Delaware River Bridge only a few minutes before. Here I was, halfway to the shore, and they weren't much past Camden Airport Circle.

I looked ahead through the haze of the propeller and saw a sparkling slash in the pine forests ahead—the Great Egg Harbor River, which I reached in the time it took some disc jockey to play one record and read one commercial on the radio.

Then, suddenly, ahead of me in the crystal clear air,

was the Atlantic Ocean, a sullen mixture of gray and green, stretching out as far as the eye could see, and directly over the hub of the propeller was the thirty-five-hundred-foot runway of the Ocean City Municipal Airport.

The engine roar dropped in pitch as I pulled on the carburetor heat and slid down in a wide spiral to make a gentle landing on the gravel strip.

The line crew topped my tanks at the gas pit while I called my wife on the phone, and, by the time we had the 140 safely tied down in the parking area, my wife and family arrived in the station wagon to greet me.

I commuted morning and night to Ocean City, far above the mob, for the entire summer (except a few days in July and August, during the hurricane season, when even the sea gulls hid). There is no doubt that the way to become a pilot is to fly consistently as much as possible and build up experience, for no matter how good a book or an instructor may be, you have to go through it yourself to learn what to expect. A good instructor can prepare you for trouble, though.

Early in my cross-country training, Bob had made me fly "hands-off" by trimming the ship with the trim tab for straight and level cruising flight, steering with my feet only. I found that, if I had her trimmed for 110 mph, and I cut the throttle slowly, her nose would drop, but the airspeed would stay at 110, or at least oscillate near 110 and finally settle down there; the Cessnas are stable.

Many times, as I bored a hole through the sky between Wings and Ocean City, I studied the chart or read the newspaper, "hands off" the controls, merely glancing around from time to time for other aircraft. People's reactions when I tell them this vary from a nervous laugh to sheer horror, for laymen seem to think that the moment a pilot lets go of the controls the wings drop off. Yet, as Bob showed me the first time up, a modern plane will fly better "hands off" than it will with a novice at the controls. Every once in a while you will read of an airplane taking off or landing all by itself with no one at the controls.

One morning I left Ocean City under ideal conditions: the dawn air was cool and clear and the weather officer at the Atlantic City Naval Air Station had told me on the telephone that visibility all over South Jersey was unlimited and that Visual Flight Rules were in operation —"It's strictly VFR all the way," is the way he said it.

On the flight towards Philadelphia the usual check points which had become old friends came into view and slid by under my wings with monotonous regularity. As I approached the Delaware River I saw that the "mountain" of smog that usually lies over Philadelphia was a lot higher than it normally appeared. If that condition appeared to me now I would call Philly Approach Control on the radio and ask them what the visibility was in the immediate area, but I didn't know enough to do it then. I used to think that the FAA Air Traffic Controllers resented private pilots calling them up on the radio. You see, I still had a lot to learn.

Thinking that this was the ordinary condition of smoke, haze, automobile and bus fumes that stagnates above any big city, I drilled right on into a fog that you could cut with a knife. Just before I hit it I had folded my local chart and turned to put it on the shelf behind me since I was only ten minutes out of Wings—practically home.

When I turned towards the front, it looked as if some

giant spray gun had coated my windshield and windows with battleship gray paint. I opened the side window and looked out. I could hardly see the left landing wheel not five feet away.

I broke out in a nervous sweat. All I could think of was spiral dives and spins that I had read killed so many noninstrument pilots when they blunder into instrument weather. I thought of making a hundred-and-eighty-degree turnback to Camden, but I was only two thousand feet over crowded Philadelphia, and I didn't want to crash into the row houses below. My instinct told me to pull back the wheel and climb into the clear blue sky above the smog where I could see! Then Bob's voice dinned into my consciousness:

"You're trimmed for straight and level flight. This smog is a purely local condition, so you can fly out of it. Take your hands off the wheel and fly straight ahead with the rudder and the gyro compass."

With tremendous effort, I forced my hands from the wheel and into my lap. They were balled up into fists, and perspiration was dripping from them as if I were holding wet rags, but the fact that I was doing something sensible ended the first flash of panic. For two or three minutes I flew thus, then the haze thinned out and there below me was the Schuylkill River, which divides Philadelphia from West Philadelphia; at least I knew where I was now. I pulled on the carb heat and sliced down to four hundred feet above the river at a hundred and twenty mph, then flew over it all the way up to Wings Field (at least there were no television towers sticking up out of the center of the river), and in a few minutes I was safely on the ground at Wings.

I told Bob about my scare. He looked pretty serious

as I recounted my experience and told me it was time he gave me a lesson so that I wouldn't be caught short by weather conditions again.

The next day I told my wife that I would be late arriving at the seashore, because I had to take a check ride. And what a ride it was!

After we strapped ourselves into the plane, Bob began to fasten orange plastic sheets over the windshield and windows, and handed me a pair of blue goggles to put on over my regular glasses. Because of the filter effect, the windows became opaque to me, although he could see through the orange plastic, since he had no blue glasses on; the fog condition was thus created artificially.

Bob took off and climbed to three thousand feet, lecturing me all the while:

"You were lucky in that fog," he said, "but don't ever let yourself get caught again like that. There are old pilots and there are bold pilots, but there are no old, bold pilots." He glanced at the skyline and made clearing turns, then said: "Now, take over and fly!"

All I could see was the panel full of instruments before me, with which I thought I had become pretty well acquainted by this time. All the needles were vibrating in the right place, oil pressure, ammeter, tachometer, airspeed, altimeter, turn and bank; and so they remained for about what seemed to be two minutes, as Bob sat sidesaddle, looking at me, a stop watch in his right hand.

Suddenly I noticed that the engine sounded a little different and glanced at the tachometer. It was 100 rpm's below the normal 2350, and the airspeed had fallen from 110 to 100 mph. I eased forward on the wheel and the needles moved to the right—the airspeed climbed 100 . . . 110 . . . 115 . . . 120 . . . 125. The tach went up, too: 2250 . . . 2300 . . . 2375 . . . 2400 . . . 2500. I brought the wheel back to slow her down and looked at the turn and bank—the needle was away over to the left. I rolled the wheel to the right and fed in some right rudder to center the needle and ball and pulled back to slow her down. The engine labored and growled, the stall-warning indicator went beeeeep, and the turn needle swung to the right. I pushed the wheel to pick up airspeed and rolled the wheel to the left. The Airspeed Indicator went up to 130, the needle snapped all the way left, and I was suddenly conscious that I was soaking wet. About this time I turned a bright yellow and screamed for help.

As he stubbed out his cigarette, Bob asked casually, "Sure you've had enough?"

"I'll tell the world I've had enough," I answered, tearing off the blinding blue goggles. There we were over on our side in a tight spiral to the left—the "graveyard spiral" they call it—the one that kills noninstrument pilots who try to fly in instrument weather. Bob looked at the stop watch that he had started when I took over the controls and had stopped when I finally gave up.

"Pretty good," he said, with his eyebrow up, "it took you twenty-three seconds—most people get into spiral dives in ten or twelve seconds."

I learned the hard way that you can't depend on your normal senses to control an airplane when you are shut off from the ground or from the horizon. You will get a strong sensation that you are climbing, when actually you are flying straight and level, so you shove the wheel to get the nose down and all of a sudden you are in a dive.

The study of blind flying or instrument technique is a

special course in itself, and someday I intend to take it, but it is by no means necessary to a private pilot who flies only in good weather.

Bob's session under the hood taught me better than all the books in the world never to take a chance with weather again and, by golly, it is a lesson well learned.

"The thing that gets me is why, when you saw a suspicious fog condition ahead of you, you didn't call Philadelphia Approach Control to find out what the situation was," Bob said to me as I brought the little plane in for a landing.

"Didn't know how to," I answered truthfully, although it made me feel a little stupid.

"O. K., you'll learn that next," he said with a big wink as he flipped off the safety belt and eased out of the cabin.

I took off for the shore with Bob standing on the edge of the field, hands on hips, head cocked a bit to one side —I knew he was smiling his crooked smile at me although I couldn't see it.

Halfway to Ocean City I noticed something. My shirt was still damp.

7. Flying Phone Booth

Out of respect for the manufacturers of modern aircraft two-way radio equipment I unhesitatingly doff my hat, hair and scalp down to my very eyebrows; without even considering its use as a navigation aid, there is no instrument in the panel that compares with it for sheer practicality and as a safety device, yet many pilots do not make use of their radio merely because no one has ever told them how to.

New pilots, particularly, shy away from using the microphone because they are afraid of being rebuffed by the government operators; fearful that if they do not use the "correct" terminology, they will be greeted upon their next landing by an ogre brandishing an official form criticizing them for daring to intrude upon the sacred wave lengths.

Few people realize that the Federal Aviation Administration maintains a nation-wide radio network devoted only to flying, the facilities of which are as readily available to the private pilot who flies a Super-Cub as they are to the professional airline pilot who flies a DC-8.

Aircraft radio communications falls into three types: the en route Air Traffic Control Centers (or as we refer to them in pilots' lingo: ATC's), the local traffic control centers situated at major airports, commonly called "towers," to flight service stations.

Most radio range stations used for navigation also have FSS voice circuits operating on the range frequency, manned by highly trained personnel (flight service specialists) who are there for only one reason: to give assistance to all pilots within the sound of their voices—routing information, weather reports or sometimes just the reassuring feeling that someone down there likes you.

Like almost everything in flying, radiotelephone technique and theory looks terribly complicated when the novice first starts to examine it. There are so many types of "in flight" or "en route" aids that the FAA issues special charts just to list the hundreds of frequencies and procedures to be used in each area: Radio Facility (RF) charts, Instrument Approach charts and Airways Radio charts are available to anyone for twenty-five cents each from the Director, U. S. Coast and Geodetic Survey, Washington, D. C., but I found that when I first received them I was overawed by the immense number of facilities operating along the East Coast. Although it doesn't hurt to have them and to know how to use them, I learned quickly under Bob Angeli that the week-end pilot can get all the radio information he needs to fly anywhere in the United States from the sectional charts, which are designed for contact flying. All you have to know is where to look for it.

After my session with the fog over Philadelphia, Bob determined to complete my radio education.

"Looky here, Dad," he said, spreading my much-battered, gasoline- and sweat-stained Washington sectional on the horizontal fin of the 140, "let's see how easy it is to use two-way radio."

His finger ran over the chart to the symbol that stood for Wings Field: WINGS 320 L H 26.

"You know that the three thirty stands for the altitude of this field above sea level. The L means that there are lights on the field for night operations, and the H tells you that there is a paved or hard-surfaced runway."

He pointed out the Ocean City Airport symbol: OCEAN CITY 8 – – 34, and continued, "The strip at Ocean City is only eight feet above sea level, has no lights and is not paved, therefore instead of the L and H they have dashes."

"What do the twenty-six and thirty-four mean?" I asked feeling like a six-year-old child.

"The last number in these symbols shows the length of the longest runway on the field in hundreds of feet: Ocean City has a thirty-four-hundred-foot runway, and the one here is twenty-six hundred feet."

He slid the chart towards me so that I could see the symbol of the Philadelphia International Airport and told me to explain it. I squinted at the information box alongside the airport and saw: 10 L H 73, then came a long series of numbers, the first printed in red, the rest in blue: 278, 118.1, 118.5, 126.18, 142.74, 257.8.

"What does that mean to you?" asked Bob jabbing at the red 278.

"Red means low frequency," I replied haltingly, "and that's the one to listen on to talk to the tower."

"That's right!" he said with a smile of approval. "Now what do these others mean to you?"

"They mean I don't know anything about radio," I

answered glumly, wondering how the dickens I could ever learn enough to feel confident about flying into controlled airports.

"You are letting your imagination run away with you because there are some things here you don't understand. What does the fact that these other numbers are printed in blue mean to you?"

"VHF," I answered.

"And what do you do with the blue numbers printed on the chart?"

"Listen to them."

"Right on both counts," said Bob with a Mona Lisa smile. "And the only other thing for you to remember is to listen to the first blue number on the chart in the radio facility box and to tell the tower that you are listening on that particular frequency, and they will come right back at you."

"What about these other numbers?" I asked, wondering how it could be so simple when I had thought it was so complicated.

"Never mind. Forget 'em. They are air-carrier frequencies and military frequencies and don't apply to you. Just call the first number and you will get along.

"One other thing—there are some frequencies that are assigned for special uses at these towers which are listed on the radio facility charts but not on the sectionals. If you are ever in doubt, call the first blue number and ask the tower for the frequencies you want to use—approach control for instance.

"Remember how you got caught in the fog last week?"

I shuddered at the memory.

"Philly approach control transmits on one two one point seven, but you can see that it is not on the chart here. Philly tower will tell you what frequency to use and you can call like this: 'Philadelphia approach control, this is Cessna seven three zero four four. Over,' and they will take you under their wing.

"Just remember to turn the transmitter selector to 122.5 to speak to a tower and to 122.1 to speak to an ATC station.

"Now, go ahead and use your radio all you want, you have your license. Don't be afraid of it. Use it just like a telephone. You don't need a lot of tricky phrases, just speak English. You'll get along all right."

Well, I didn't use the transmitter right away. Mike fright, I suppose. I flew around listening to the chatter on the radio when I was near a large airport or to the voices of the ATC boys moving airliners around the sky as though playing a three dimensional game of chess, and while doing so, picked up a lot of the lingo and began to feel at home with it. But the mike hung on the hook unused until one day when I really needed it, and —well, it was this way:

My good friend, Dr. E. H. Vick, who treats my children on an assembly-line basis for everything from sun poisoning to fractured skulls, had a cabin in the Pocono Mountains for the summer. Since my three boys are extremely active, gregarious, brittle-boned and susceptible, Dr. Vick spends a great deal of his waking time at our house, and therefore it seemed only fair that his beautiful wife and he should invite my beautiful wife and me to spend a restful week-end in the mountains—without the children.

The law business being what it is, I couldn't get away on Friday morning, so my wife drove ahead to the mountains, the plan being that I should fly up as soon as I got free at the office.

To shrink a long story, I didn't break loose until one o'clock Saturday afternoon, and it was almost two by the time I checked the 140, strapped it on, and took off for Mount Pocono. The weather report was good with six miles of visibility, but there were a lot of fluffy clouds about three thousand feet up, and, as I scooted along five hundred feet below the cloud base, I became aware that the clouds and I were holding our own, but that the rolling hills were rising increasingly higher and higher toward us. I didn't want to climb up into the clouds, because Bob's lesson had had its effect on me, but, on the other hand, the average cloud is softer than the average mountain, and I was beginning to worry that they were eventually going to meet. Go ahead or go back? Why guess? That's what the FAA is for! I dug out the chart and looked for the frequency of Allentown Range somewhere to the left ahead of me, which I finally found in the blue box next to the station. I clicked the communications selector to "Comm," and tuned in to the call signal "ABE." The visibility was getting down to three miles now and I was just skimming along under the cloud base, when I ran into the goldurnedest rainstorm you ever saw.

The rain came in through the ventilators like water out of a hose and my coat, the charts and the seat next to me were drenched before I could turn the airscoops around. I said a few things that would be inappropriate in a church, pulled the carburetor heat on, and looked around to see where I was, meanwhile trying to dry the chart off with my handkerchief.

I could see straight down and to my right, but upwards, ahead and to my left the air was full of falling sky juice; I couldn't see the Delaware River off to my right any more so figured I must have wandered eastwardly over to New Jersey while monkeying around with the ventilators and the wet wash. All the while I could hear the radio monotonously going "dit dah, dah dit dit dit, dit" and I wished I had read those articles on orientation problems a little more closely.

I flew north out of one shower and into another, wondering if the engine was going to drown, when suddenly a flash came to me to turn the omni bearing selector to center the VOR needle. When I did it, the word "FROM" came up in the little window at the bottom of the dial, which confused me; I still couldn't figure whether I was over Pennsylvania or New Jersey and although I knew the electronic gadget was trying to help me, and that I was on *some* VOR radial, I still didn't know which. Then I realized that Bob had told me that when the needle centered the little window should show a "TO," so I rotated the knob until the needle was re-centered with the friendly "TO" smiling at me. The numbers on the omni bearing selector showed a "33," indicating that I should fly a 330° heading and keep the omni needle centered to fly towards the Allentown VOR. Although I was still flustered—confused is the word—I flipped a mental coin and turned left towards the station figuring that I would soon see something familiar. My guess was good. In about two minutes I came to the Delaware River which located me. I turned right and followed the river towards the Water Gap, about ten miles away. Of course I still had the cloud versus mountain problem unresolved, but I was happy to solve one problem at a time.

Then I found out for myself the hardest thing about using a radio transmitter. It is picking up the mike and pressing the button for the first time. Talk about mike fright—I was so affected that I couldn't get up nerve to press the button for five minutes and, when I spoke, it wasn't my normal voice at all. It sounded more like a record that has been played too fast, all squeaky and run-together. "Allentown Radio, this is Cessna seven three zero four four. Over."

The Allentown range answered me promptly but told me to stand by; there were other calls on the line. For another five minutes I flew into the lightening atmosphere, then finally the range said:

"Cessna seven three zero four four, this is Allentown Radio. Send your message."

"Zero four four on contact flight to Mount Pocono," I answered. "What is the ceiling and visibility up there? Over."

No answer.

I said it again.

Finally the voice came back: "Zero four four, your signal is unreadable, you must be too low over the mountains. Out."

That was my first experience talking on the radio, but it was enough to break the ice. Although it did not help me on that trip I was never again hesitant to pick up the microphone and call anyone, so I guess it was a valuable experience, although I didn't think so at the time.

Incidentally, everything worked out just fine, the cloud cover stayed at three thousand feet, and when I finally got to Stroudsburg I flew at fifteen hundred feet up Brodheads Creek which I have fished from one end to the other since I was old enough to stand in the cold water without crying, then followed the roads I know so well right into Mount Pocono Field.

The next morning I stopped in to Harold Kreck's store in Mountain Home to buy some dry flies and heard him complaining to another customer about some "damn fool pilot" going over his house the previous afternoon and waking his kid up from a nap. I assume he was referring to someone else, but I didn't stay around to inquire.

As the hours mounted in my log book I picked up more and more information about radio. In addition to tower and range frequencies printed on the charts there are other VHF channels assigned for special uses which are not shown thereon.

Metropolitan tower operators are generally busier than a policeman at an Irish picnic, making clearances for planes taking off, landing, separating traffic in the pattern, filing and closing flight plans, so the primary tower frequency is literally a hot line. The FAA has therefore assigned a separate frequency called Ground Control to be used only for controlling aircraft on the ground, for taxiing, parking and general policing of the area. At almost every large airport this frequency can be heard by the pilot on 121.9 megacycles, thus taking a lot of the message load off the tower frequency. Some, though not all, aircraft transmitters have the frequency in their transmitter (121.7 megs) for talking to the ground controllers, but if you do not have it ask for information on the tower frequency and listen on 121.9. This is how you would use it:

Suppose you are on the Atlantic Aviation ramp, Philadelphia International Airport, in a Bonanza. You get in, run a preflight inspection, start the engine and turn the VHF receiver to the ground control frequency.

Before you can move one inch on a controlled airport you must have permission from the tower, so you click the transmitter frequency selector (which is controlled by a separate crystal for each frequency) to GC-121.7 and call:

"Ground Control, this is Bonanza eight zero zero four delta. Over." ("Delta" is the phonetic alphabet word for "D.")

The overhead speaker squawks as you fine-tune the receiver to 121.9: "Bonanza eight zero zero four delta, this is ground control. Over."

You press the microphone button; "Zero four delta on the Atlantic ramp. Taxi instructions for take-off, please. Over."

"Zero four delta cleared to runway nine."

You answer "zero four delta," to let them know that you have heard them, open the throttle a bit and roll slowly around the huge airport building over the tremendous expanse of concrete apron, past a loading DC-9, then come up beside a Boeing 707 waiting to taxi into one of the gates on loading Pier A, its big engines slowly idling. You hit the brakes, pick up the mike and say:

"Ground Control, this is zero four delta. Will you tell the boys in that 707 not to start those jets until I get past? Over."

"Trans World seventeen, there is a Bonanza passing behind you. Don't rev her up until the small plane is beyond your left wing tip," squawks the speaker.

"Trans World seventeen, Roger," says a faint voice.

Then the voice in the speaker says, "O. K., zero four delta, go ahead."

You open the throttle and roll four hundred yards to the end of runway nine, stopping on the taxi strip about a hundred and twenty-five feet from the runway, à la regulations.

After you have checked the mags, set the prop pitch, and run the trim tab to "take off," you turn the selector—click-click-click—to 118.1 megacycles. Up comes the mike to your lips:

"Philly Tower, this is Bonanza eight zero zero four ready to take off on runway nine."

"Zero four delta, hold your position," orders the tower, so you answer, "Zero four delta," and sit there, engine ticking over, until a DC-8 comes in for a landing on the runway ahead of you. Before the "Dizzy-eight" is half-way down the runway, your speaker blares,

"Zero four delta, take the active and hold."

You say, "Zero four delta," and ease the Bonanza out on the big white "9" of the active runway, point the nose down to the other end—and wait.

By the time the DC-8 has turned left to waddle like a big bird to Pier A, the Voice says, "Zero four delta cleared for immediate take-off."

"Immediate" from a tower means immediate, for there is probably another big plane on final approach, landing on runway nine after you take off, so you ease the throttle slowly all the way forward, and press the microphone button.

"Zero four delta rolling," and in a few seconds you say, "Request permission to make a right turn out. Over."

"O. K., zero four delta, cleared to make right turn out of pattern, have a nice week-end. Out."

Radio is so nice—you don't have to keep feeding dimes into it.

A few years ago the FAA and FCC approved a VHF channel for communication between private planes and private airports only. Those stations, properly called "Aeronautical Advisory Stations," are more popularly

known as "Unicoms" and both transmit and receive on
122.8 megacycles. This is a nice crystal to have because,
often on a cross-country, you will see a small airport on
the chart and wonder if they might have a restaurant,
overnight facilities, or mayhap a restroom, so you can
swing the selector knob to U and call "Jamestown Unicom, this is Piper one four two three Charlie. Over."
When they answer, you get the info you need. Also relief.

Not long ago, I flew a Tri-Pacer from Wings on a hurried business trip to Washington, D. C. (my beloved
Cessna was in the shop for its annual relicensing at the
time). On the way home, about five thousand feet over
Wilmington, I turned on the Unicom frequency to tell
Wings that I would land in about twelve minutes. Since
122.8 is a "party line," I listened before I started to
transmit and, sure enough, someone was talking:

"West Chester Unicom, this is Cessna. . . . Over."

Then I heard another voice, not quite so loud, say
"Cessna . . . this is Apache. . . . Over."

"Go ahead, Apache, is that you, Joe?"

"Yeah," said the Apache, "where *are* you, Charlie?"

"About five angels [five thousand feet] over New Cas-
tle. Where are *you?*"

"I have ten over Harrisburg, going to Pittsburgh. See
you tomorrow at the first tee?"

"Roger," said the Cessna, then: "West Chester Unicom—anyone home?"

A new voice broke in "West Chester here, go ahead."

"This is Charlie Blank, call my wife and tell her to
pick me up."

"Roger," said the newest voice, and then the line was

free for me to call Wings, which, by this time, was in sight anyhow.

Another special frequency is 121.5 megacycles, the "emergency" frequency, not used very often, but available as a clear channel for people who are in need of immediate assistance. If you feel in dire need of someone to hold your hand and lead you out of flight problems, you merely click the channel selector over to "E," transmit "blind," and pass your message. All ATCs, towers (both military and civil) and Coast Guard stations listen to, or "guard," 121.5 constantly, even though it is not listed in the little boxes printed on the sheets, and they are with you pronto on the same frequency.

There are a couple of nice features about 121.5, apart from real emergency calls: You can be found when you are lost; on 121.5 you can call radar and direction finding stations.

I was flying with a friend in his Cessna 170 B from Youngstown to Philadelphia one day when the visibility seemed to be getting worse and we decided to land until things got a little better. There was a slight detail—I was lost, as usual. Bob says I am a versatile pilot: I can get lost in *any* airplane. I knew we were somewhere over the mountains of western Pennsylvania, but didn't know exactly where, so I tuned in 121.5, picked up the mike and said,

"Tiny Tim, this is Cessna six five two four Baker. Over."

"Tiny Tim" is a code word used for calling for assistance from ground radar stations who watch air traffic. After two calls a voice came back:

"This is Tiny Tim, what is the matter?"

"I am on Visual Flight Plan to Philadelphia and am slightly lost. I want to land before the weather gets any worse."

"O. K.," said the young man somewhere in the hills below, crouched over a radar screen, "make a left three sixty standard turn." I hadn't fooled him a second with that "slightly lost" stuff.

I put the needle one width to the left and watched the sweep second hand on the panel clock. As the second hand hit "60" for the second time, I felt the plane tremble—I was passing through my own turbulence from two minutes before—and the speaker said,

"I have you good and sharp. You are about eight miles north of New Bethlehem, not far from Victor thirty. What do you want to do?"

"I want to land," I answered, trying not to sound too anxious.

"Take heading of two two four, on the Pittsburgh VOR. In fifteen miles you should see the Allegheny River. If you have any trouble, call again. Good luck. Out." We knew where we were now.

As I swung around to two hundred and twenty-four degrees and tuned in the Pittsburgh VOR, I looked at the chart; on the west side of the river there was a fifteen-hundred-foot runway at McVille Airport. We rode the VOR radial until we saw the river, then looked down and there was the field. We landed, had a cup of coffee and a cigarette and, when the weatherman smiled, took off again for an uneventful trip home.

Often the facility information boxes relating to towers have the letters "DF" in them. Direction finders operate, also, to find you when you are lost, as long as they can *hear* your transmission. You call the nearest ATC or tower and, after establishing communication and telling your troubles, talk into a live mike so the "DF" boys can use their radio loops to "home" on your voice; as soon as two or three of them lay fixes on the source of your transmission, the point where the lines of bearing converge is where you are. All you have to do is talk for a minute or so. If you are really lost, I suggest your monologue begin: "Our Father . . ."

Even a guy like me, for whom it is easy to *get* lost, finds pretty hard to *stay* lost—or even become bewildered, with radio equipment.

One two one point five has another use, too, which is sanctioned by the FAA. Suppose a private pilot has to contact a military tower which does not have civilian frequencies. Use 121.5, of course! All towers and ATCs have it, so in a pinch you can talk to them, even if they have no civilian frequencies assigned on the charts.

When *real* trouble comes, the word is "MAYDAY," which comes from the French, "M'aidez," or "Help me." It is the aerial SOS and has absolutely top priority over all other messages.

Late one afternoon during World War II, thousands of student-pilots were returning to their home airport in Texas after a full day of gunnery, bombing, navigating and simulated combat, from all over the State of Texas. They were tired, red-eyed, low on gas, and anxious to get back on the ground. There were so many planes aloft that one could see two entire landing patterns entering the two parallel runways, one left-hand and one right-hand, with the BT-13's stretched out like so many beads on twin strings indicating the paths used to enter the pattern, the downwind and base legs, the approaches and the taxi courses to the ramp. There were never less than three planes on each strip at one time—one landing, one rolling out, and one turning off onto the taxiway. It was frantic.

The boys in the tower were talking a mile a minute to get all the planes cleared and landed before it got dark, when suddenly the routine of calls over the tower speaker was shattered with an electrifying message: "Tower, this is Flight zero zero zero—*MAYDAY*."

The two controllers looked at each other in horror, then the call went out, "This is the tower. There is a Mayday in the pattern. Clear the area immediately."

Instantly the precisely formed lines of planes dissolved into a maelstrom of bees on the swarm, as every plane turned out of the pattern—it was every man for himself getting away from the field.

The controllers rushed around their big glass room, searching the sky for a limping plane, or a smear of smoke, but there was nothing to be seen, anywhere. The senior controller flipped a switch and spoke: "Mayday, this is the tower. Where are you? We don't see you. Over."

Back came a querulous voice: "Sir, this is Cadet Blank, on taxi strip four. I have run out of gas."

It took two hours to get the incoming planes straightened out, and I never did find out what happened to the poor cadet who called Mayday, when he was safe on the ground. Boiled in oil, probably. Slowly.

A while back I related my experience of plunging into a blinding fog over Philadelphia, and how Bob taught me to avoid repeating such a dumb stunt.

Any time you are near a big city airport that has GCA

(Ground Controlled Approach), your light plane will be picked up as a point of light on their scopes along with the big commercial jobs that they are routing through the congestion. Even on otherwise clear days, if there is a lot of smoke and haze over the city, so that the visibility may be down to minimums in the area, I now believe in keeping in touch with Ground Controlled Approach. Using the proper frequency I call: "Philadelphia Approach Control, this is Cessna seven three zero four four receiving on one two one point seven. Over."

When they come back I say, "Zero four four three thousand feet over Camden heading three three nine, airspeed one one zero. Can I pass through Philadelphia to Wings?"

"O. K.," Approach Control may say, "we see you. It's clear to pass through." Sometimes they say, "Hold over Camden; there is a Convair landing from New York." Then, after a few minutes, "Zero four four, you are cleared to Wings."

Having talked to Approach Control on the radio from my flying telephone booth, I decided to go up in the new Philadelphia Air Terminal building to watch them at work one rainy day.

The radar room, about twelve by twenty feet in size, was hung all around with thick draperies to keep out light and noise. Over on one side the gloom was washed back by the eerie light from two radar scopes, in front of which were seated three men—one sitting directly before each glowing scope and the third man between and slightly behind them. They all had microphones. It kind of reminded me of the witch scene in *Macbeth*.

The left radar screen showed all air traffic in the area

for a radius of twenty-five miles from Trenton to Wilmington. The other showed the landing glide path area for runway nine only. The faces of the scopes were about twenty inches across, and from the center a white line rotated like a sweep second hand, except that it took only three or four seconds for each complete sweep. Outside, the rain was coming down in sheets, yet there were seventeen pinpoints of light on the twenty-five-mile scope—each one represented an airplane worth a million dollars and carrying from fifty to eighty passengers hurtling through the air at three hundred and fifty mph, completely blinded by the rain and fog; but they were safer than you are in your car when your vision is momentarily blinded by the glare of oncoming headlights. The "eye in the sky" watches every one of those planes, plots its course, orders it to rise or descend to certain altitudes and keeps them separated and policed as positively as you can move chessmen on a board in front of you. Is it any wonder that these controllers would be disturbed when, under haze or smoke conditions, a small plane comes into the area covered by the radar and doesn't get in touch with them? They say it is like looking down from a hotel window and seeing a small child crossing the street in the middle of traffic—they see it surrounded by danger, but they can't do a thing about it.

So I call in on the radio, let them know who I am, and where I am, and they take me under their wing. There's no rule that makes me do this, but it makes a lot of sense to me and, as I said before, I am the cautious type.

In speaking over the radio there are certain distortions to human voices and you should use certain uniform procedure to avoid misunderstandings and unnecessary repetitions that clutter up the party line.

For example, experienced pilots don't say "A, B, C." Instead they use what is called a phonetic alphabet, as in "Able, Baker, Charlie," the one I learned in the service, or "Alfa, Bravo, Coca," the one some bureaucrat foisted off on us when we weren't looking. In practice, you can use either or, if you forget, you can still say, "A as in Airplane," just so the tower understands you. But it's not professional.

There is a regular pattern of radiotelephone phraseology, most of which will sound familiar if you have young children who watch television.

"Stand by," "Say again," "Negative" (for "No,"), "Affirmative" (for "Yes"), and similar words are all self-explanatory. Never say, "Over and Out," or you tag yourself as the rankest of amateurs.

"Over" is used when you expect an answer. "Out" means that your end of the conversation is finished. They don't fit in the same sentence.

A word that has become a part of the language is "Roger." This is the phonetic alphabet word for "R," and indicates that the last message has been received and understood. It is a formal word, not to be treated lightly. If you don't understand something, never say "Roger." Instead, ask the sender to "Say again the last message."

There is a story about a very stuffy officer dressed in Air Force Blue and wearing a shiny new star on each shoulder, who was making an inspection of an Air Force Base control tower as a flight of F-84D's was being landed by the tower operator. The last "dog" turned on its base leg and the enlisted operator cleared him to land. Back over the loudspeaker came a happy voice, "Roger-Dodger."

The General stiffened at the breach of proper radio technique, seized the tower microphone and said, "Air Force Jet, use the correct phraseology!"

Again the pilot's voice came back as he turned on final and dropped his flaps and gear, "Roger-Dodger."

The General turned brick red and snarled into the mike, "This is General Glip, use the correct phraseology!"

The jet flared out in a flawless landing and the speaker said, "Roger-Dodger, you old codger, I'm a General, too!"

8. Flight Plans

By this time I hope to have made one point clear at least: a pilot is never alone, even though he may be flying solo, as long as he has two-way radio. The eyes and ears of the FAA are always at work for the benefit of everyone aloft.

The phrase "Flight Plans" sends some so-called aviators into a case of the shakes. I know of one private pilot who has logged several hundred hours, yet has never filed a flight plan. "No cops are going to tell *me* how to fly," he says, stamping his feet, which makes little puffs of smoke come out of the hole in his head. He doesn't realize that filing a plan is simply a notification to the FAA of his flight pattern from take-off to landing, giving the time he expects to arrive at his destination. If he doesn't arrive, or for some reason doesn't notify the FAA of his arrival, someone goes looking for him along his course line. Submitting a flight plan is for the protection and assistance of the private pilot; the FAA is not a cop telling him where or how to fly. Under conditions where the visibility is better than three miles in controlled areas so that the Visual Flight Rules (VFR) are in operation, you don't have to file a flight plan; but no matter how clear the weather is I never go anywhere without filing one.

The regulations are clear—the only pilots who must file flight plans are the instrument-rated pilots who fly when they cannot see more than a mile; then Instrument Flight Rules (IFR) apply and these pilots file plans so that their flights can be spaced, controlled and separated by the Air Traffic Controllers in order to avoid collisions in the air. Remember those radar boys and the points of light on their scopes? When the conditions go "below minimums" and the weatherman chants "IFR," that's when we private pilots sit home and watch television, anyhow, so let's forget IFR flight plans.

When the weather is CAVU (Ceiling and Visibility Unlimited), why file a flight plan? The answer is simple logic.

Before you leave on a cross-country, you have already marked the course on the chart and planned your flight pretty well—where you will go to pick up a range, where you will refuel, where you will land if your destination is "socked in"; in other words, you plan every flight, just as you plan a trip into the city or a trip to the grocery. So why not tell the FAA about it? It's so easy. The FAA has a regular printed form called a flight plan which you can use in three ways: You can fill the form out at a FAA station or tower and leave it with the radio room; you can call them on the telephone and say, "I want to file a flight plan," and they'll ask you for the pertinent information if you have no form to guide you; or, you can do the same thing by radio. but it is not recommended because the circuits are usually pretty busy around a big city. Incidentally, you call a Flight Service Station for this purpose—their numbers are listed in every telephone book under United States Government and will be found under FAA Flight Service Station, sometimes with the remark "single call pilot briefing"—and they pass the word along the route with your "eta" (estimated time of arrival) so they will start chasing you down if you are late or overdue.

The flight plan is simple and is on a printed form available at all FSS facilities and at most fixed base operations; it starts off with the type of flight plan, VFR or IFR, the number on your aircraft, the type you are flying, the true airspeed, point of departure, time of departure, cruising altitude, route of flight, destination airport, estimated time en route, fuel aboard and your name and address—just in case.

When I called in, it went like this: "VFR . . . Cessna seven three zero four four . . . Cessna one-forty . . . 105 miles per hour . . . departing Wings Field at zero nine hundred, local time . . . Cruising VFR at three thousand feet, direct to Niagara Falls, New York . . . Estimating one two three zero [1230, or 12:30 p.m.] F. K. Smith [address] two people on board with four hours fuel. Airplane is silver with red trim."

If you are going to do it the easy way and ride the electronic airways, for your routing you would say, instead of "direct," "Wings to Williamsport, direct, thence Victor three one to Buffalo."

Then, as you proceed, you can give position reports to the Flight Service stations: "Elmira radio, this is Cessna seven three zero four four, VFR Philadelphia to Buffalo, past Elmira at three zero [thirty minutes past the hour] estimating Buffalo in one hour . . ."

Suppose you have not called in to Buffalo to close your flight plan, and the time you estimated for arriving has slid by. Your flight plan on the clipboard at Buffalo begins to get warm. If another twenty minutes goes by, the FSS man in Buffalo begins to check.

First, he calls all of the fixed base operators around the Buffalo/Niagara Falls area to see if maybe you have landed and simply forgotten to close the flight plan, either by radio or by telephone. If no one knows anything about you, he will start to call back along your route to see if you have reported past or made a radio contact (all of which are logged by N-number).

Pretty soon, a call goes in to the Civil Air Patrol to stand by for a Search and Rescue Mission along your route, and in another hour, the CAP is brought to a full SARCAP alert and the massive search for the lost aircraft gets under way. The costs a whale of a lot of money, but it is provided for every pilot who files and opens a flight plan! So you can see how important it is, not only to file but also to close that flight plan when you arrive at your POD—point of destination. All you have to do is call on the radio (or on the telephone when you get on the ground) and tell the FSS, "Close my VFR flight plan on N-73044."

No, you are certainly not alone up there, and you can see that the guy who resents flight plans as some kind of intrusion on his privacy has some pretty backward ideas about flying.

9. Week-end Pilot

On a hot summer afternoon I returned from the hundred-mile cross-country jaunt that FAA requires and took my flight log to my instructor for his inspection.

"Well, Dad," he said, after leafing through the little book and handing it back to me, "it's time you went to Allentown and took the FAA examination for your private pilot's license. Tomorrow morning would be a good time."

I felt like an Ancient Birdman by this time—I had all of thirty-nine hours and twenty-two minutes logged in, mostly over the Jersey pines.

The following ack emma, I took off from Wings, climbed into the brilliant sunshine to three thousand feet, put the compass needle on 003 and flew, happily and carefree, listening on the radio to recorded dance music from New York. I felt cocky and self-sufficient, which I should have recognized as a bad omen on the basis of past experience, and drilled along looking occasionally at my wrist watch to see how close I was getting to the Allentown-Bethlehem-Easton Airport, which nestles in a bend in the Lehigh River, five miles north of Bethlehem, about twenty-five minutes from Wings.

For fifteen minutes everything was enjoyably routine. The scenery was beautiful, the air was smooth, and the C-85 settled into the hum that I recognized as the cruising rpm of the little airplane. I patted the instrument panel and winked as I nodded towards the engine, whence came the sound—"Listen, baby," I said to the plane, "our song." The world, it seemed, was my apple.

A few miles south of Bethlehem I noticed for the first time a huge pall of smoke hanging over the area, and, as the propeller chewed into the atmosphere, I became aware that the visibility was becoming more and more restricted. This wasn't nature's murk, this was strictly man-made. The steel mills spread all over the landscape were being worked full blast and each was putting out immense billowing clouds of acrid smoke. It came into the cabin and made my eyes burn, and I choked as it went into my lungs. Worst of all, it clung to and obscured large areas of the ground and, as I had not been to Allentown Airport since my first flight with Bob, I wasn't quite sure of the terrain in general, and the location of the field in particular. The apple, it appeared, was going bad.

I looked at my watch and saw that we should be "there," so I switched the radio from "BC" to 122.5, tuned the receiver to the tower, "snicked" the mike off the hook, and called Allentown Tower.

After a pause of about half a dozen heartbeats, the headphones crackled: "Cessna seven three zero four four, this is Allentown Tower. Over."

Well, I must be close to them to hear them this clearly! I pushed the mike button again: "Zero four four over

Bethlehem at three thousand, landing at Allentown. Instructions, please. Over."

"Zero four four cleared to enter traffic pattern for runway six. Call on base leg."

"Zero four four, Roger," I answered doubtfully, because I couldn't see more than 10 per cent of ground now and that not too clearly. I opened the window and peered down at the gray blanket as I made a lazy left turn. Suddenly, there below me, through a hole in the smoke, I saw the characteristic asterisk-shaped pattern of crossed, paved runways. With a quick look around for other traffic, I rolled her into a steep bank, pulled on the carb heat, cut back the power, and spiraled quickly down through the hole. In a short time I had sliced down to one thousand feet, under the smoke level, slid into my downwind leg and reported to the Tower, "zero four four on downwind."

"Roger, zero four four," was the bored answer. When I arrived at the end of the runway, I turned left ninety degrees onto base leg and reported again to the Tower.

"O. K., zero four four. Cleared to land on runway six."

I acknowledged and turned onto final approach. Once more I picked the mike off the hook. "Zero four four on final," I said, as I throttled back and dropped the flaps with over a mile of flat paved runway stretching out ahead of me. Twice the headphones made a funny hissing noise, as it does when someone holds down a microphone button, then a plaintive voice came through: "Zero four four, where *are* you? We don't see you!"

I took my right hand off the throttle knob and scooped the mike from my lap. "Zero four four is about to touch down at the end of runway six," I said, wondering why the heck they couldn't see me this close to the tower.

The airspeed was sloughing off and the stall warning indicator had made a couple of preliminary beeps, so I was easing her onto the strip, when the voice came back, "What *color* is the runway?"

I pressed the button and said, "White," as the concrete blurred and we began to sink in. I dropped the microphone on the empty seat beside me and heard the wheels go "chew-chew" as we touched down at fifty-five mph.

"Our runways are black," said a disgusted voice in my headset. "You are landing at the wrong airport!" Yikes!

I shoved the throttle forward, kept rolling in a "touch-and-go" and got right back into the smoky air, humiliated and disgusted. Here I was on my way to take my FAA exam to be a pilot, and I landed at the wrong airport! I very nearly turned around and went home right then and there.

Then the voice on the phones said, "Zero four four, do you still read me?" I answered that I did.

"You were at Convair Field six miles away. Climb to one thousand, take heading of zero three seven for four minutes, enter the pattern and call on downwind leg for runway six."

I did as they told me and soon saw the crisscrossed black runways through the arc of the propeller, as I wheeled into the pattern and called the tower, "zero four four, one thousand, I have the field in sight."

"Are you *sure?*" was the response. I could sense amusement in the voice coming from the tower there below me, and realized that my miscue was nothing unique to the controllers. The banter made tension run off me like water off the proverbial duck's back, and I gaily answered, "Affirmative. Head up and locked. Request permission to land immediately before I get lost again."

"Cleared to land immediately runway six. Land short and take first exit right."

I slid into the extreme end of the paving in a short-field landing and turned right at the first turnoff. Then I saw what the tower men were doing: the rascals made me taxi right past the tower so they could give me a ribbing. Not to be outdone, as I rode past, I removed my headphones, ostentatiously doffed the baseball cap I was wearing and bowed as low as my safety belt and the small cabin would permit. Up behind the big tinted windows three faces cracked into broad grins, and my bow was returned in kind; then the face on the end was obscured behind a small black object and I heard the headphones on my lap crackle, "Welcome aboard. Glad you finally made it!" In a moment I was past them, but it is a moment I will never forget, for that was my first realization that tower personnel are real, human, down-to-earth guys, who want to help you, not crack the whip over you as if you are an aerial tramp.

The flight test and written exam were given, marked and graded in three hours, and I returned to Wings with my certificate marked "Private Pilot—Qualified to fly single-engine land planes with passengers."

When I received the certificate showing that I was a genuine private pilot, Daddy finally got some prestige around the Smith household. At the insistence of the three boys, we had a family celebration, which culminated with a name-the-plane contest. The winner was to have the first ride.

I viewed the proceedings with some alarm, because my little mob is name-happy. I didn't quite know exactly what to expect, since we have an assorted group of pets cluttering up the house, all of whom have been formally named by contests: a dog named David, a parakeet named Rocky, a rabbit named Cyril, a turtle named Myrtle and a cat named Irving. Who could possibly guess what colorful handle the kids would dream up for the pretty little 140?

After a caucus in the powder room, the boys returned with their unanimous choice and a drawing of a "figurehead" for luck—it seems that son No. 1 was reading *Moby Dick* at the time.

The name—*Legal Eagle*—was not too spectacular, maybe, but better than Irving, and the drawing was perfect: a bedraggled, disreputable, simple-looking bird, with a vacuous expression and sporting a great wig like those worn by judges of the English courts.

The contest having ended in a three-way tie, the next day everyone had a flight with Daddy. I don't know who got the greatest kick out of it. Yes I do, too. I did.

As a licensed private pilot, the wraps were off. I was allowed, for the first time, to fly when and where I pleased carrying passengers—if I could find passengers who would go with me, that is. I hadn't thought much about this problem because, while I was flying as a student pilot, I had many people say, "When you get your license take me for a ride sometime, will you? I've never been up." Then I found, almost universally, when the invitation did materialize, they had lost their interest. Suddenly something had come up and they couldn't make it. Too bad. Next time, maybe.

There was one potential passenger who didn't have to be coaxed—my oldest son, aged thirteen. He and I flew together every free moment of daylight for the rest of the summer and every week-end when the weather was good. This, in itself, was a wonderful twist, because I had been so busy in my preflight days being a "successful" lawyer that I had neglected to be a proper parent, but strangers no more, we were like a couple of kids together, flying around the Eastern United States with the same interests, for the first time of our lives.

On a series of week-ends we relived and learned the history of the United States that he had been studying in school, far better than he could learn it out of a book. We flew to Boston and followed the ride of Paul Revere from an altitude of fifteen hundred feet. We flew over Bunker Hill and Boston Harbor. We saw where Washington crossed the Delaware River to attack the Hessians at Trenton, and the Civil War's bloody battlegrounds at Savannah and Gettysburg.

We saw where the *Monitor* fought the *Merrimac,* and where Jefferson lived as a boy. We saw New England tobacco farms and Southern cotton plantations and Jersey truck farms and Ohio wheat fields. We flew over prairies and mountains, swamplands and fishing fleets. "America, the Beautiful" means something to us now.

We flew the length of Pennsylvania's Susquehanna from Conowingo Dam to Hallstead, and we cruised New York's lush Hudson Valley. We looked down on the Atlantic coastline and the Great Lakes; Niagara's Gorge and the Nation's Capital. To us, James Fenimore Cooper's Indians again peopled the rolling hills cut through by the ancient waterways, the routes of the first Americans. In an hour we covered more distance than a birchbark canoe could cover in a day, and saw more of the verdant country in a day than an Indian saw in his lifetime.

Why, oh, why, are people satisfied to travel along highways or railroads and think that they have seen our wonderful country? No one touring in a car can capture the feeling of a New England town off to one side of the road, with its white churches and its common, or realize how a river and its tributaries dominate and control the growth of an urban area. I pity the poor driver who concentrates only on the rear end of the car ahead of him and the car behind, reflected in his mirror; he can't even see as much as the passengers—at least they can survey the billboards and trees and service stations alongside the road.

Do you wonder, then, that I am happiest when flying; that for me every flight is a new insight into the country that I have been so close to, yet now realize that I have never known?

My memories of these flights are filled with snatches of beauty, each distinct, yet all run together, until I get out the logbook to review the notes on each individual jaunt. There is one trip that will always be clearly remembered no matter how long I live.

My son and I drove to Wings on a Saturday morning at about 0730, planning to fly up the edge of Long Island Sound to Newport, Rhode Island, then across Buzzards Bay to Falmouth on Cape Cod, then all along the outer curve of the Cape to look over the beaches for surf fishing, stopping for lunch at Provincetown, thence home. It was a typical week-end trip for us, and we took off as planned, after checking the weather, filing a flight plan and inspecting the airplane. I had the New York and Boston sectional charts in my lap, while climbing slowly and, therefore, was not particularly interested in

looking at the scenery until we were trimmed for cruising flight. At 0800 I trimmed her out at five thousand
feet, where we were supposed to have a tailwind, and
picked up the southwest leg of the Newark range.

We had hardly reached cruising altitude over Prince-
ton University, when we saw the most electrifying sight
I have ever seen in my life. My whole body broke out in
goose pimples the size of ping-pong balls. There, thirty
miles ahead of us, off a mite to the right, washed in the
golden morning sunshine, absolutely clear and free from
any trace of the usual ground haze or smoke which usually hides it, lay greater New York, a concentration of
eight million people, like a relief map. As we came closer
and details became clearer, we could see Manhattan with
both the Hudson and East rivers spanned by many
bridges that seem, from the air, to keep the island from
floating away. The Bronx and Brooklyn spread out before us like painted scenery and far below tiny water
beetles moved slowly in and out of the myriad docks and
slips that serrated the river front on both sides. We saw
how the biggest skyscrapers rise in clumps in the down-
town end of Manhattan, the Fifth Avenue shopping center, and along Riverside Drive. Stuyvesant Town and
the United Nations looked like architect's models over
on the East side. And Central Park! I had never realized
how big the lake is in its northern portion. For the
first time I saw how the diagonal slash that is Broadway
cuts like a scar across the orderly man-designed paral-
lels of blocks in the center of the island. I could imagine
its beginning as an Indian trail long before some shiny
beads changed hands. At five thousand feet even the towering Empire State Building looks pretty puny. I had

been on that congested strip of real estate hundreds of times, but never had I seen it as anything but a maze of man-made canyons.

Now I saw it for what it really was—a tremendous community that had begun and grown, because of its waterway communication, to such a size that its commerce supports millions of people. No longer a mishmash of dirty, crowded streets, policemen with white gloves, smelly busses, harried pedestrians, noisy taxicabs, grimy theaters, tinsel bars, plush hotels, New York was for the first time seen as a full length, soft-focus picture, instead of a composite of close-ups showing enlarged pores, blemishes and smeared make-up. Despite my past impressions, she had suddenly become beautiful, distinguished and dignified all at once, a city to be proud of.

We flew, in an hour, over the New England coastline to Cape Cod and had lunch. That afternoon, as we flew homeward bound, I took time to drop low over the Hudson River and curved right at the Upper Bay so we might pay our respects to America's girl friend, the Statue of Liberty. I swear that, as we went shooting by, free as a bird, she winked at us!

With each week-end tour out beyond the edge of the world, I gained still more confidence in the 140 and, as a result, my flights went to points progressively farther from our home field, for it is in cross-country flying that pilots have the most sheer fun out of aviation, and, while relaxing aloft, learn more and more about the art of flying as they use up pages in the logbook.

The weather isn't always clear and sunshiny either, but one learns to live with it.

Rain, when I first started to fly, had always scared me,

because I thought that it would get into the engine and make it stop. But my first Mount Pocono trip had taught me that rain is not harmful to the engine; on the contrary, it makes it run cooler and better. In fact, it improves combustion and smooths out its operation.

No, it is not rain, *per se*, that causes the trouble; it is, rather, the restriction to visibility from the spattered windshield and especially the strong and gusty winds or turbulence that occurs around thunderstorms and makes it imperative to get down on the ground until the sun comes boiling through again.

Thunderstorms, unless there are a lot of them, needn't keep you grounded, for they generally occur in the late afternoons during the summer months, are slow-moving and usually intense over a relatively small area. As a rule, if you see them, you can run around them the way you walk around a puddle on the sidewalk. Just don't get into them, that's all! From the air thunderstorms usually look like gray slanting columns topped by huge towering thunderheads—sometimes with jagged sparks of lightning flashing around them. I know, because I met a bunch of them at one time, and it was something like being mugged in an alley.

It was a hot, humid August afternoon. I was flying solo to Ocean City, having been first advised that the weather was all right for contact flight, although there was a possibility of local thunderstorms all over South Jersey later in the afternoon and evening.

Passing over Clementon at thirty-five hundred feet, I saw what seemed to be thunderstorm activity thirty miles ahead of me, somewhat south of my course. As I purred along, I kept my eye on what now appeared to be a line of storms, rather than one storm—which I

could have outrun. As the propeller augered into the atmosphere, I realized that there were two thunderheads
about five miles apart between me and Ocean City; calculating that I could fly between them, I swung south
into the trough of clear air behind the first one. That
was a mistake. It soon became clear that number two
and I were on a collision course. I again swung around
to get out of the area and turned the VHF radio
on to pick up the half-hour weather broadcast from
Millville Radio. It was no good; crashing static made
reception impossible. I snapped off the set, removed the
headphones, put them back on the shelf and tried to
think how I could pick my way through the marching
columns. By now it was getting bumpy, storm number
two was only a couple of miles away, and lightning was
flashing to the ground and inside the storm itself. I
turned right to run away from it and stole a look at the
compass which was whirling like a dervish and wouldn't
settle down in the rough air. Then, to complicate matters, I saw a third storm looming up ahead of me. Suddenly the windshield was streaked with rain and the air
got really rough. I was in the edge of the storm now, and
thinking of lightning, I racked around in a right
hundred-and-eighty-degree turn, and pulled on the carburetor heat, just in case. Whoops! There was another
storm! I was boxed in and couldn't run away because
the bumpiness had made me slow down too much. Although the 140 normally cruised at a hundred and ten
mph in calm air, I eased off the airspeed to avoid over-
loading the wings, to soften the bumps, just as you take
it easy on a rough road in your car. The airspeed
dropped down to 90, and my pulse was the same. About
this time it became clear, even to me, that I was in the

wrong place at the right time, and that I had better get back to earth. I looked down from the rain-streaked window, hoping to see some place to land, but nothing was in sight below except the pines of Jersey, crisscrossed with narrow dirt roads. Since I was south of my regular course, I didn't recognize any landmarks. Furthermore, because of the errant compass, I wasn't sure which way was north; my twisting, turning flight had completely confused my sense of direction. To complete the picture, I was lost!

Then below me I saw some tiny cows, and I concluded that, where there are cows, there must be a pasture. I put the 140 in a vertical spiral to lose altitude fast, and took a quick appraisal of the terrain. It looked pretty flat and free of boulders as I slid past downwind at four hundred feet, so I turned into the wind, throttled back, dropped the flaps and headed for the near edge of the green field. This was to be a pasture landing, but I knew that it wasn't going to be tough, for in practice I had flown out of many airports that were laid out on steeper grades than this slice of gently rolling greensward. The fact that this amounted to a "forced landing" never occurred to me; as far I was concerned, it was just a routine safety measure to avoid the storm that I knew was dangerous. The airspeed dropped to 55 and the swaying pine trees were only a few feet below me when I chopped the throttle at the edge of the field and settled in on the close-cropped grass. I don't think that I rolled three hundred feet. As the first few large drops of rain splattered on the windshield, I taxied to the windward edge of the pasture, cut the switch, clambered quickly out, drove my metal stakes into the ground and tied her down. In a minute the rain fell in torrents and the wind blew branches out of trees, but I sat snug and dry in the 140, rocking gently in her tie-down ropes as the water sluiced down the twin blue-tinted skylights over my head. I wondered if my wife was worried. (She was.) I kicked myself for getting caught like that in a storm. But Bob had been right again, as usual: in modern light planes, even when you blunder stupidly into problem weather, you can call it a day, pull the flaps and set her down safely on a pasture, a golf course or a beach. Any port in a storm.

Twenty minutes later the rain stopped and it became light outside. I swung down to the soggy ground, untied the ropes from the struts and tail wheel and pulled up my stakes. A walk-around inspection showed that the plane was all right, so I hauled the tail around to turn the 140 towards the pastoral runway, wetted a finger and held it up to see which way the wind was blowing.

As the sun burst out in its full glory from behind the clouds, I saw how short the pasture was and the shadow of a doubt as to whether I could make it flitted over my mind; but since I had made many simulated short-field take-offs with Bob, I figured I could make it. I pulled the tail of the plane back as far to the edge of the field as I could, with the nose pointing into what little breeze there was, got in, and started the engine. Stepping hard on the toe-brakes, I checked out the mags, dropped the flaps two notches and opened the throttle all the way. For five seconds I held her there, while the plane vibrated and shook as the C-85 roared in a power build-up; then I released the brakes and eased the wheel forward. The tail came up and we began to roll; the airspeed indictator broke loose—40 . . . 45 . . . 50 . . . 55—she was airborne; but, instead of climbing immediately, I held her down close to the grass, building airspeed as the pine trees ahead got closer and closer, then I eased the wheel back a few inches, and the fast-moving plane fairly leaped over the trees that seemed to be clutching at us. I felt like a high jumper as we soared over the pines and climbed into the blue. Every time I take off I feel as though I have been drinking champagne; sort of bubbly and tingling all over. This time it was pink champagne.

When my originally timorous friends saw that my son and I returned safely from our week-end tours, their nervousness receded and one by one they began to approach me sheepishly, asking if they could go for rides. Needless to say, as I filled their requests, they became enthusiasts like me, and what a whale of a time we had on our magic carpet.

We flew, in the late summer, to Cape Cod to fish in the surf for striped bass, and to Upper New York State to fish for trout. We flew to Virginia and North Carolina to shoot ducks in the fall, and twice I hunted pheasants with friends over two hundred miles from home, yet was able to squire my wife to parties in Philadelphia the same evening, fresh as a daisy.

I did all the things I had wanted to do for years that a tight schedule would not have permitted, had it not been for the airplane. I could cover two hundred miles in the time it would have taken to travel sixty or seventy miles in an automobile, and, at the same time, since I was recharged with the enthusiasm of youth, I was able to turn out more work at the office than I ever had before.

There is nothing that will enhance a parent's life like doing things with his children, and the airplane made this possible, too.

As I have said, my thirteen-year-old number-one boy, King, usually accompanies me aloft because, after they are ten years old, most boys cease being "Mother's boys," and tend to grow closer to Dad. But the little boys want to fly on week-ends, too, and I indulge them as often as possible.

I have carried many passengers of different ages and sexes, yet none compare with young children. Kids take to the air as naturally as they take to riding in a car. They are not afraid of it, I suppose because they see so much of it on television and in the movies. And you should see their faces light up when they look *down* and see clouds for the first time.

My smaller sons, Doug and Greg, usually accompany me, one at a time, when the other has a social engagement or a doctor's appointment. I try to keep the trips short, so they won't get restless—nothing over a hundred miles—just far enough for them to work up a thirst or an appetite.

Without offering any apology, I confess that I am ham enough to love to taxi up to a parking space next to a spectators' area and watch the expression on people's faces when a seven- or eight-year-old shimmies to the ground from the right-hand door of my Cessna. But the youngsters never notice the spectators; they just take my hand and lead me to the nearest soda counter, for which they have an unerring instinct, and load up on all those things that spoil their dinner and make their mother mad at me.

Besides three sons, the pattern of my life is ruled by

the whims of the large woolly black dog named David, a standard French poodle boasting a better pedigree than most people I know. He cuddles with my wife, all sixty pounds of him, goes duck-hunting with me, and wrestles with Doug and Greg all day long, which has him completely confused mentally. He is not sure whether he is a lap dog, a hunter or a little boy.

Having given the boys rides at Wings on a nice fall afternoon, I was preparing to tie the plane down and call it quits. My wife was waiting for me on the ramp, talking to big, genial Frank Mayock, the general manager of the field, and holding David on a leash. The pup barked frantically and began jumping and squirming, trying to come to me; then his collar snapped and suddenly he was free. He cleared a four-foot wire fence like a bird, ran at the *Legal Eagle* like a black streak, and vaulted into the cabin, where he sat apparently waiting for his turn to go round the pattern.

I slid into the left seat to see what he would do, and he nudged me with his nose and looked out of the windshield. I closed the door, called "Clear," started the engine, and he began to quiver with excitement, just as he does when he sees me get my shotgun out of the rack. Although I had my doubts, I waved to my wife and taxied down the strip. She shook her head resignedly and Mayock grinned at me. When I opened the throttle to take off, David's tail was wagging faster than the propeller revolved, his eyes sparkled, and he swung his head around with a herkey-jerkey motion, ears flying out like a girl's pony tail.

As we took off, he cocked his head to one side at the receding ground as if to say, "Hey, what's going on here?" then, as we climbed to four hundred feet, he sat back with a panting "grin" and obviously enjoyed himself. I had another passenger.

David now has about thirty hours aloft under his belt. He usually sits with his nose pressed tightly against the air intake ventilator, moving it away only when he sees birds or other airplanes, at which he howls and barks excitedly, as he does at other dogs when he is riding in the car.

One day, with David flying "co-pilot," I landed at Mercer County Airport near Trenton, taxied over to the fence, parked, and went into the hangar to make a telephone call, leaving him alone in the plane.

When I came out there was a family of four children and their parents, watching airplanes taking off and landing, which everyone seems to like to do. As I approached whistling, David, who had been lying flat on the seat, sat up with that erect, alert look which poodles have, looking for me through the windshield, and the woman grabbed the man's arm in alarm.

"Goddlemighty," I heard her say, "look at the face on *that* pilot." Then, after a frozen silence of three or four seconds, the man breathed, "Let's go home." Amid a tautly strained silence, the parents gathered their brood to their bosoms and hurried them to the family car, which quickly disappeared on two wheels, tires screaming in protest. I wish I could have heard their table conversation at dinner that night!

10. New Fields to Conquer

Many years ago, while participating in a field trip as a student of geology, I had the phenomenal luck of finding, for the first time in that part of the world, a dinosaur footprint millions of years old that upset a lot of scientific theories on saurian distribution. My finding the print was purely an accident, for the professor had sent me out to gather some gangoric fish fossils (whatever they are) and, besides, I didn't even know that the relic I carted home had any value; I thought it was merely an enormous fern leaf. Anyhow, I got my name in all the papers and was a sort of minor celebrity around college for two or three days.

Although that small hunk of mud-turned-to-stone is my sole contribution to the field of science, the glamour surrounding the entire episode kindled a small flame of desire down deep in my boiler room—a desire to be someday an explorer, an archeologist, an adventurer. But after college came law school, and marriage, and war (this has nothing to do with my marriage), and three children (this has), and it soon became clear that my only voyages of exploration were going to be vicarious, from reading books such as *Kon-Tiki* and *Search for the Lost City*; my active life as a working explorer was curbed by the insatiable demands of my children for food, clothing and shoes, unreasonable as it may seem.

Then I got the Cessna 140.

With the airplane at my disposal, a new world opened before me—as if I were a latter-day Aladdin with my own private genie, who would carry me over mountains, plains, rivers, forests and cities quickly, safely, as I should command. I was free of the restrictions of time and space which had bound me to an area of a few miles from my home; a two- or three-hundred-mile flight takes less than three hours and, with a three-hundred-mile operating radius, I could explore on my week-ends a quarter of a million square miles of the northeastern part of the United States.

An explorer is defined as one "who travels over a strange new region and returns to report on what he has found," so some of my pedantic friends made fun of my "explorations."

"New lands?" they would chortle . . . "strange places?" It was a laugh to them because they knew that I have lived in Boston and Hartford and Washington and Niagara Falls—a laugh, that is, until these scoffers began to fly with me and learned for themselves that from the sky the world is a new place. From aloft the very neighborhood in which you were born and raised becomes strange; what once seemed to be the beginning and the end of the world suddenly appears in its true perspective, as a small part of the tremendous whole.

Perspective! That is perhaps the most dramatic impart of flying for, as you fly higher and higher, the little details fade into insignificance; at the same time the background expands without limit, and the effect is much the same as gazing at the stars, in the dark of the moon, far from the glare of the city. It puts you in your place.

This change in perspective plays tricks on you sometimes, until you learn to cope with it.

There is a famous old Pennsylvania landmark on the west branch of the Susquehanna River, named Bald Eagle Mountain after a crusty old Indian chief who, it is reported, used its top as a lookout position. When I was about sixteen years old I climbed to that lookout spot to see the view. The fact that I was exhausted and bruised from head to toe by the time I reached the top generated two extremely persistent opinions in my mind: first, that the crest of Bald Eagle Mountain was an extremely high point; and second, a sincere doubt that the old chief ever used the lookout point himself. He probably sent the Indian equivalent of a second lieutenant with orders to report back if anything came up.

On a recent flight to Williamsport, I told my oldest son, who was navigating for me, about the big mountain used by the Indians who controlled the Muncy Valley and, in remembrance of my climb, made the thing sound like the second cousin to Mount Everest. Stories, with me, lose nothing in the telling.

The kid's navigation was perfect. We crossed the Selinsgrove range, and saw the river make a dip towards the east, then reverse itself and shoot off abruptly to the west a few miles ahead of us.

We were both looking for the mountain located in the bend of the river but, from six thousand feet, all we could see was farm land. No mountains. No Bald Eagle.

No Hairy Hawk. No Nothing. Only farm land. I felt like someone who has just discovered that his pocket has been picked, and my son's repeated eyebrows-high side-long glances didn't help. But it was a matter of perspective—from six thousand feet the fifteen-hundred-foot mountain, as high as the Empire State Building, was nothing but a low, rolling hill. It was not until I had descended into the bend of the river to land at the Williamsport Airport that Bald Eagle loomed high to the south of us, and proved to my son that I hadn't been making it all up.

There is more than a change in optical perspective from an airplane, for it has an enormous effect on one's mental perspective as well. You begin to see everything differently; life itself is seen from a new viewpoint.

Frequently I must go to Harrisburg, our state capital, and, before I had the plane, I drove my car on the magnificent Pennsylvania Turnpike at seventy miles an hour and faster, a real scorcher. I never stopped to think that people get killed doing that.

Now I fly *over* the turnpike on my way to Harrisburg, free as a bird, not hemmed in or restricted by features of the terrain: mountains, rivers, cities; I pass over them without stubbing my toe or getting my feet wet and, as I fly directly, I can see the white dual super-highway drift off to my right out of sight, then come cutting back at an angle passing to my left before it crosses the river south of Harrisburg. Looking down, I see tiny automobiles inching along more slowly, apparently, than ants, although I know that they are pushing their cars to the limit of the law, and beyond. Faster, faster, speed, speed, go, go—we drive our cars and live our lives the same way, at the same frantic tempo, and from a plane it seems so silly, for you can see the concrete highway stretching out for miles behind and ahead of the speeding cars. Whether they go ninety miles an hour or fifty, the course they will follow will be the same, undulating across the rolling foothills of the Alleghenies. Sort of makes you feel like God, looking down on the poor humans and seeing our past and our futures while all we can see is the blurred present. Maybe God looks at the man who is overworking himself and says, "The road is ahead of you to be traveled, but enjoy it. Relax. Slow down and live longer."

With the Cessna as my steed, I became an explorer—of sorts.

From my reading of history I conclude that there are two kinds of explorers: first, the navigators—beards and all—who spent their lives plying the uncharted seas, not knowing where they were or where they were going, until they ran into something solid; and, second, the cautious, clean-shaven types, who, from a known position, explored bays, rivers, sounds and estuaries, returning home occasionally to give the girls a whirl and pick up a few bucks on the lecture circuit. The latter type of exploration appeals to me, because exploring waterways gives you something definite to follow; like stories, they have beginnings and endings. And there are so many of them.

Where did this river begin, what effect has it had on the countryside and where does it flow finally into the ocean? It is a fascinating game finding the answers to these questions, and there is no way to find them that compares with flying.

In many respects rivers have lives and personalities just as people do. They may start humbly or gloriously, from a spring welling out of the earth, or from a large body of water, such as a lake. They may grow in stature, in beauty and in strength or they may become corrupt, ugly and degenerate. They may flow a few short miles or a thousand. Every one is different, whether it is the Connecticut, the Hudson, the Potomac, the Delaware, the Mullica or the Susquehanna—and I have explored them all.

My logbook shows that in less than one day my son and I flew the length of the Susquehanna, the major river of central Pennsylvania. I remember distinctly that it was a nice day, clear, balmy and with excellent visibility; the few puffy clouds at thirty-five hundred feet cast shadows on the earth below from the sun shining overhead. The trees were in bloom and multicolored fields were gold and green, like a chenille rug spread out as far as the eye could see.

We began our exploration at a little community named McGee's Mills, about thirty-five miles north of Johnstown, where the Susquehanna first becomes a definable river (west of the Mills there are many streams winding their way through the meadows, but no one of them, from the air, can be pointed out as the beginning).

The river here was really little more than a trout stream, shallow, full of rocks and stone bars, rimmed with trees, its sparkling waters shimmering like a narrow band of rhinestones. We dropped down to five hundred feet (legal over open country) and swung along, following a generally northeast course.

From time to time we saw fishermen standing hip-deep

in the stream, casting for trout or bass, and they looked up at us as we whizzed by overhead, their white faces showing clearly in the bright sunshine.

In a few minutes the hills began growing higher, and the river suddenly seemed deeper, for its surface was as smooth as glass and occasionally we could see canoeists and boaters who waved in response to our dipping wing. The names of the towns we passed over are romantic— Lumber City, Woodland, Clearfield, Paddy Run, Driftwood, Drury's Run, Lock Haven—lumbering country, this. The hills are still full of standing timber, but there are also unsightly gashes, mementos of the wasteful past. Lumber and the rivers. . . . I told my son how, years ago, they used to float huge log rafts down this waterway to build the cities we would soon see downstream.

Then bridges, one of the first signs of civilization, appeared ahead of us like hurdles on a track: truss bridges, wooden bridges, steel bridges, concrete bridges, one-arch bridges at first, then three arches as the river broadens, and then, at Lock Haven, where the river is a half-mile wide, a long concrete bridge crosses the river near the Piper Aircraft factory. Hide the code books, here comes a Cessna spy!

We hopped over the Lock Haven span and dropped down near the surface, skimming along all the way to Williamsport, where we looked up at our old friend, Bald Eagle, to our right; then, with a shove on the throttle, in two minutes we were flying over the mountain, south, towards White Deer. The river was no trout stream now; it was growing lusty, as hundreds of small streams poured into it; but now there were parasites sucking strength and cleanliness out of it, mills and factories drawing up thousands and thousands of gallons of the clean blood of the river for use in industry. At least they don't pump acids and refuse back in return as they used to do, vile, noxious concoctions that killed the fish and poisoned the water all the way to the sea.

On each side of the river there were spidery, black lines that swayed to and fro as the river bent this way and that, the ever-present railroad tracks following nature's level. The tracks never strayed far from the river and occasionally crossed it on mile-long viaducts and trestles. Our stream had become a roaring, frothy race in some places, yet still limpid and beautiful in others. More bridges slid by under our wings: steel truss bridges, black and gray and silver and rusty red.

From five thousand feet we saw that the river had done an amazing thing: rather than flowing parallel to the line of hills, it had cut through them almost at right angles, leaving high stone bluffs as scar tissue which showed through the covering of mosslike trees. We saw farm land again and dropped down to see the fence lines, clearly defined by rows of trees planted by seed-carrying birds and uncut for many years; apparently the dimensions of those fields are not going to be altered quickly. The banks of the main stream were lined with huge old shade trees, standing shoulder to shoulder, guarding the farm land from the river like so many policemen. No doubt some of those trees were here before the Indians were.

There to the right the railroad tracks were now four instead of two, and finally grew into a marshaling yard; there must be a city ahead. Yes, there's the smoke and haze that spells "city" to an airman. A city? An anthill, rather. A dirty, jammed-together conglomeration of angular, ugly buildings which affront the eye after the clean, pastoral beauty upstream, but in a minute we flashed past and the river flowed again through checker-board farm land. My son pointed ahead and asked: "What's that ugly building?" I didn't know. A hotel? Certainly not a hotel standing out there all by itself in the middle of these fields. Then we saw the strings of railroad hopper cars, and realized that we must be over a coal mine and the huge eleven-story building is a coal breaker, built years ago when coal was king in Pennsylvania.

The cities were coming more often now, and they were bigger and uglier. Each takes something from the river and each returns something to it.

Farms again, separated by the mile-wide river, frequently crossed by the inevitable bridges and the remains of bridges which have finally succumbed to the inexorable push of the water sixty seconds every minute, forever. And the river "just keeps on rolling along," usually calm, sometimes sullen, never really quiet.

Highways were swinging into the pattern of the river, first two-lane, then three- and four-lane, as required by the gradual increase of traffic.

The river was much wider now, and there were sand bars on the outside of many of the curves, gravel and sand piled up by the relentless water-flow of millions of years.

The hills were steeper here and higher, full of heavy woods, for this is still lumbering country, some of it virgin forest.

We slid over another city lying athwart the stream, its east and west portions connected by spidery bridges; then, a few miles below it our stream was joined by another one, almost the same size, and we had a full-fledged river at last, two miles wide in places. My, how our baby had grown!

Another city—a big one this time—Harrisburg, with yacht clubs, power and sailboats racing out in the middle of the river, and public bathing beaches and broad drives on either bank, shaded by tremendous old trees. The railroad tracks were never far away, though. From three thousand feet we could see the yards and junctions over to our left behind the city.

There were hundreds of islands in the river here, some large, some too small to sustain plant life. We saw a cluster of tents—a Boy Scout encampment—and we dropped down and saluted them, circling the camp while the boys waved shirts, canoe paddles and flags, then we leveled out and in a moment they were left far behind.

The river was not twisting and turning any more; it seemed to have sensed its destiny. Like a broken-field runner in the clear, it headed directly to the sea and, in a few more minutes, we zipped over Conowingo Dam with a highway crossing its rim and saw the mouth of the river, a mile wide, funneling into the Chesapeake Bay.

We had seen the pattern of life itself: starting from almost nothing, the river had grown in stature and strength, finally flowing into a larger life that has, at first, no apparent connection with the stream so many miles away.

"Why fly a river?" people ask me, "they're all the same." Such people are to be pitied for their cynical outlook. Rivers are as much alike as girls are alike, and the average man is always giving the girls the "double-O" no matter how many he sees. I do—wife or no.

Why fly a river? For the same reason men climb mountains. Because they are there. And because it is the greatest kind of fun, this river flying. For a few hours you can follow in the footsteps or paddle swirls of Cadillac, LaSalle, DeSoto and, in Illinois, Lincoln. Next year I am going to "fly" the Mississippi!

The "bearded navigators" had a point, too, which we quickly found in our sport of light-plane flying.

The reverse side of the sectional charts are crammed with information of every type and description concerning flying: routing, emergency signals, phonetic alphabets, radio procedure—all kinds of pithy stuff—but the trap that repeatedly catches me is the list of "aerodromes," as they call them, a word that always reminds me of Spads, Fokkers and Eddie Rickenbacker, for some reason.

Wings Field is situated on two charts: at the top of the Washington sectional and at the bottom of the New York sectional, and their combined lists of "aerodromes" totals three hundred and forty-five, listed like this: "Name —West Chester; position by Latitude and Longitude: 41° 07'-73° 42'; Elevation 380 feet; number of runways —2; length of longest runway—2200 feet; surface of runway—sod." Again and again the airports have their surfaces described—sod, turf, sand, gravel, shale and turf, conditioned and turf, bituminous and turf, turf and bare, turf and cinder, turf, turf, turf.

So a new flying "game" was invented to while away the nice week-ends, sort of a cross between "pin the tail on the donkey" and "hide the weenie"; we call it "Where's the airport?"

The first step of the game is to get a sectional chart with our own airport on it, turn to the aerodrome list and, closing one's eyes tight, put a pencil point on the list. The second step is to fly to the airport thus chosen, the only restriction being that we can't go to the same place twice. This is not too difficult a rule to comply with because, with all the "sod" fields on the list, often we don't get to the same place even *once*, which, of course, adds to the general merriment if it ever becomes known around our home field. The reason for this consistent difficulty in finding the sod airports is their natural camouflage; they blend into the background unobtrusively like a praying mantis on a rosebush, or a flounder on the bottom of the sea; hence, the name of the game. I respectfully suggest that, if Civil Defense people want effectively to camouflage towns and cities, they paint them to resemble private airports.

As one approaches the general area, he can cheat a little by peering around the sky for low-flying aircraft that look as if they are fixing to land, for that is usually the easiest way to find the field. The only trouble with this is that over farm country you may see several planes in the air at one time, all diving into cabbage patches and berry bogs—the crop dusters at work. One time I blithely followed an Ercoupe around a pattern and landed close behind him, only to find that I had followed a flying farmer almost into his barn, which cost me two demerits.

With another pilot along as observer, you can't be too anxious to follow any plane; you work carefully into the area and begin to peer surreptitiously at the ground, looking for long streaks of tire marks, bare spots, and especially bright colored planes marked wing to wing, the best tip-off that you have arrived. If there are no planes in sight, you are in trouble: you go around and around looking down at hundreds of oblong fields that

could be the airport, but aren't, with all those cows loll-
ing around. Then suddenly, just as suddenly as you see
the mantis on the bush and wonder how in the world
you could have missed it before, there is the airport, its
close-cropped grass inviting you to sit her down. Smugly
you cut the throttle, pull on the carb heat and head in
for a Coke, or coffee and doughnuts.

Why do we enjoy our game of "Where's the airport"?
First of all, there is the pure euphoria of flight itself,
which is a major part of the game, and the second is the
fun we get out of playing any game of skill: to test our
navigation and our technique of approaching and landing on a new field, with its special problems and individual characteristics, for the hundreds of fields listed
on the back of the sectionals are similar, yet completely
individual, like so many fingerprints. And there is an
enormous satisfaction when you make a perfect approach
to a new field, and come in to a flawless landing—more,
I think, than the satisfaction of sinking a thirty-foot putt
or coming about the mark perfectly in a sailboat race.

Then you ease out of the plane to stroll into the office
to do a little "hangar flying" with the boys, which may
go on for hours, for flying is more than a means of transportation; it is a way of life to those engaged in the aviation business, whether they are pilots, airport operators
or salesmen. They eat, sleep and live flying twenty-four
hours a day. They will sit on a bench in the spring sunshine with their backs against the office wall and watch
landings and approaches and, if you bounce on landing,
as we all do once in a while, the railbirds are sure to
comment when you taxi in to the gas pump.

"Don't forget to log two landings on that," they will
say, out of the sides of their mouths. And if you

taxi around with your flaps down, you have to buy everyone on the field a cup of coffee. You only do it once, and that's enough.

The moment you are listed with the FAA as an "Airman"—the day that you receive your student's license—you become a member of an exclusive club, and when you come onto a strange field, you are accepted into the group; even though you don't know anyone, you feel at home. Everyone is friendly and helpful and usually bends over backwards to help you, and no one is trying to gouge the last dime out of your wallet.

If you want to stay somewhere overnight, as you would on a long trip, you can leave your plane tied down outside on the line as long as you want, usually without charge. And even the smallest fields seem to have tie-down rings in the ground and to supply ropes to anchor the plane against the weather. Hard as it may seem to believe at first, a properly tied-down airplane can withstand severe gusts of wind without suffering any damage, although trees may be blown down, house roofs deshingled and power lines put out of commission. The secret, if it can be called that, is to tie the plane tautly and not leave anything loose to bang around. Aileron, flap and tail-assembly locks limit movement of the control surfaces and prevent damage. I have one serious reservation, though: I don't trust regular airport tie-down ropes any more; since they usually lie around in sun and rain, they rot and become weakened, so I always carry three or four ten-foot lengths of good half-inch manila in the back of my plane, along with a set of five metal stakes. The best kind of manila or nylon rope that can be purchased at a war surplus store for a fishcake is the greatest insurance in the world against those sudden windstorms that come up out of nowhere, and woe be it if the rotten airport ropes give way!

I will never forget one terrible afternoon on a crowded country airport when I hung for dear life on the right wing-strut of my 140 as the chill wind blew a gale and the rain bucketed the area almost horizontally. As I clung there, drenched to the skin, I saw a gorgeous Cessna 120 three spaces away, rocking violently due to slackness in the tie-down ropes. Suddenly, the rope on the right wing snapped and the wing blew up, up, up— and the plane lifted like a giant kite, straight up on its tail; the left wing's rope also snapped, and then the plane went crashing over on its back, with a twisting motion that bent both wings as if they were made of tin-foil. The plane lay there in the gale for a moment, shuddering like a wounded bird, until the wind got under the tail and flipped it up on its nose, where the full force of the blow acted on those broken wings. The stricken 120 cartwheeled between two rows of parked planes, grinding itself to pieces before my eyes, with a series of bangs and crashes like a set of pots being thrown downstairs. Just as it got to my 140, it flopped for the last time; the windstorm had departed as swiftly as it had come.

The 120 was a total loss, except for the landing gear and wheels. The fuselage was twisted like a piece of taffy; the windshield, both side windows and skylights were smashed; the battery had split open and acid was all over the instruments; and the rain had drenched everything in the cabin. The prop was ruined and the brand-new Continental engine, with only eighteen hours on it, was good only for junk. All because the tie-down ropes snapped from being slack and weakened from age.

So I carry my *own* ropes—I *know* they are strong.

One question frequently asked of me concerns the cost of landing at various fields, and most people are surprised when I relate that in my experience landing "fees" are very rare, and, in fact, are usually charged only at the largest municipal airports. I can't say I strenuously object to them, because I am willing to pay for the facilities at a big airport. Besides, you aren't usually taken unawares; the sectional charts carry this sort of information in that box on the back of the chart where all the aerodromes are listed, saying: "LDG FEE." Then you can decide whether it is worth it before you go in. You take your choice and pay your money, you might say.

There are exceptions to this generalization, though.

One time Tom and I were on a cross-country over a pretty desolate area, I think it was Virginia. That morning we each had thought that the other would bring along some sandwiches for lunch, and neither of us had done so; that, as they say, is life. It was almost noon. The marker for the left tank indicated below one-fourth so I turned the selector to the right tank and began to think of taking on fuel for the plane and ourselves. As I flew, Tom began checking the chart for an airport nearby.

"There's one," he said, pointing to a spot on the chart just ahead on our position, and we began to scrutinize the tree-covered terrain before us for a cleared space. For a few minutes we searched around until finally I saw a fairly open area about two thousand feet long and pointed it out. Tom squinted at it, then looked at me strangely.

"What are you, nuts?" he asked. "That's a gravel pit."

"Well, let's drag it and see," I said, admitting to myself that this certainly was no Idlewild. We dropped the flaps, slowed to sixty-five mph, and went down the area at an altitude of fifty feet, looking it over. There, on the top of a dilapidated building, was a tattered windsock, which I showed to Tom.

"Well?" I asked.

He crossed his arms and growled, "I still say it's a gravel pit."

We slid over the trees and eased onto the "runway," making small stones spray from the wheels and rattle against the metal fuselage like a charge of buckshot. Tom turned to me and said, "See?"

Then we saw the goat. It was tethered to the door of a large doghouse, munching on a piece of garbage or something, for there wasn't any grass around. As we taxied past the run-down hangar towards what looked like a gas drum perched on a rack, a seedy-looking man, needing a shave, sauntered out.

"Do you have eighty octane?" I asked, killing the engine.

"Yep," he said, drowning a fly in a splash of tobacco juice; then, so help me, he put ten gallons of gas in the plane, one gallon at a time, using a rusty tin can which he filled with a hand pump from the fifty-gallon drum. He balked like a steer when I demanded that he strain it through a chamois, but finally conceded the point. With the tanks full, I gave him five dollars, expecting the gas to cost about three-eighty, but, to my surprise, he handed me a mere ten cents change.

"How do you figure that?" I asked, looking at the lone dime in my palm.

"Simple arithmetic," he said, as if talking to an idiot child. "Ten gallons at thirty-eight cents a gallon is three-eighty; ten cents for the chamois, makes it three-ninety, and a dollar landing fee. Four-ninety from five dollars leaves ten cents." We got out of there before he charged us the remaining dime for parking.

Another time, Tom and I landed at Westchester County Airport, just above New York City, on our way to Boston. It was our first time into that field, which is very busy since it is used not only by private and business fliers and some of the smaller airlines, but also by National Guard jets on the week-ends.

We landed and were cleared by the tower to park over by the fence at the spectators' section. As we unjacked the headphones and unfastened our safety belts, a yellow pickup truck came roaring up the line and skidded to a stop in front of us.

"They sure give you service here," I said to Tom, as the driver leaped out of the cab and ran around to my open door.

"Fill up both tanks," I said grandly.

"Sure, sure," said the driver, making a face, "but first there'll be one dollar, landing fee. I looked at the back of the chart and saw that there was no indication that a fee would be charged, so, before the poor guy was finished, I made him clean the windshield, pump up the tires, check the battery, fluff the seat cushions and pull the prop over.

"That'll be one dollar's worth of landing fee," I said to Tom as we got cleared to take off. He laughed. He's mean that way.

There are some places that you couldn't possibly pay any landing fee: several of my friends land on river sand bars to fish in the stream. I have always been the kind of person who lets the other fellow dive into the water first to test its depth, so the only way I would land on a bar is after someone else showed me it was safe, but I have lots of pictures of their outings and the fish they have caught. And, aside from regular airports, there are many other natural landing places available for light planes: farms, beaches, and, if need be, roads.

I have seen airplanes on the Jersey beaches often at low tide, the pilots casting into the surf a hundred feet away and, in some parts of the farm country, it is unusual *not* to see a light-plane strip with a Piper Cub or Aeronca parked next to the other farm equipment.

Several air strips between Philadelphia and Miami are maintained and operated by motel operators, spread out for sky-tourists' normal stops, and the same thing is true out West, where flying seems to be more popular than it is in my part of the country. These stopovers make air-touring pleasant and comfortable, so I always plan to stay at them when I go on a long trip by my plane; I don't want to scrounge into any old field or flying farmer's strip and take my chances on overnight accommodations. I like clean sheets and a soft bed, not a haymow or cow palace, which is what you usually end up with, despite the plethora of farmer's-daughter jokes that we all have heard. Now I plan my overnight stops as I did when I used to take trips by automobile. In those days I first called the AAA and got a "routing slip," which showed me how to go and advised me on the best places to eat and stay overnight. Now I do the same thing whenever I am going to fly overnight, for I belong to a flying club which operates just like the AAA, the Aircraft Owners and Pilots Association.

The AOPA was founded about 1940 by an energetic group of private and business pilots who were afraid that private flying was going to be pushed around by the commercial airlines and the military, and was based on the idea that "in unity there is strength." It is a great outfit to belong to, and costs only ten bucks a year.

Before I take any extended jaunt, I write to AOPA for help, and they send me routing information, special FAA regulations I may encounter, and tell me where to stay; all I have to do is to file a flight plan accordingly. Touring by air can be done "first class," even in a light plane.

Moreover, as a member of AOPA, one has other facilities available to him.

One of the most frequently expressed criticisms of private flying is that you have no mobility on the ground once you have reached your destination, that flying is a practical example of what we called in the Navy, "Hurry up and wait." This, too, has been changed to a large degree. AOPA members can rent Hertz and Avis "Drive-it-yourself" automobiles with no red tape, merely by showing the credit cards that come as part of their membership. I can fly to almost any big city, rent a car right at the airport, and have all the freedom of transportation I could have with my own car. More. My wife doesn't have to borrow it.

There is an "air-charge" card, too, on which one can charge gas, oil, batteries and repairs, and pay later on a billing, which makes it unnecessary to carry money all the time. Besides, the critics of private and business flying are not aware of another advantage held by light-plane fliers over the passengers on large airplanes: We can usually land close to the city we want to visit for business or for pleasure, and don't have to take an hour's journey from the outlying commercial airports with their unobstructed seven-thousand-foot runways.

In Chicago, for instance, I land at Meigs Field, an island right out in Lake Michigan, not ten minutes from the Loop. Washington, D. C., Miami, Detroit, Philadelphia, all have light-plane fields close to wherever you want to go, clearly marked on the charts, away from the main airline terminals.

As part of our game of "Where's the airport?" we have landed on all kinds of runways—some of them flat, others seemed like roller coasters—and never had any trouble. A few surprises, maybe, but no trouble; just new fields to conquer.

Taking off in an early spring thaw, we once rolled through a quagmire going about fifty mph and the silver airplane suddenly looked as if it had been smacked with a gigantic mud pie. The side windows and most of the windshield became opaque because of the congealed gumbo, which quickly dried into a sheath of dirt as the slipstream evaporated the water. We flew to the small airport that was our "field to conquer" that day and located it fairly quickly, despite the dirty windows, because it was bracketed between a river and a highway. As we turned onto final approach and let the flaps down preparatory to landing, I saw ahead, squarely in the intersection of the crossed sod runways, a large slick area which I assumed was ice, and held the wheel back to ease onto it as gently as possible. It wasn't ice; it was water, and the 140 landed with a splash that could only be duplicated by dropping a grand piano off the Golden Gate Bridge. It did the trick, though; the plane sure was washed clean fifty-nine seconds faster than in a "minute wash."

One Saturday morning we were picking our airport for the day, when some other air-loafers strolled into the waiting room from the coffee shop.

"What's up?" asked one of the fellows who had told us a few minutes before that he was going to take a couple of friends for their first plane ride in his Tri-Pacer.

I took a deep breath, trying to frame an answer that would lend some dignity to the childish game we played, and decided I might as well make a clean breast of the whole thing. I explained our method of selecting new fields to conquer, and braced myself for a blast of guffaws which never came.

"Why didn't I think of that?" said the questioner, reaching for his Pennsylvania aeronautical chart which Pennsylvania pilots get free from Harrisburg. He closed his eyes, put his finger on the big list of airports, and he and his two passengers eagerly crowded over the chart to see where they were going.

"Lehighton," crowed the pilot, laying the chart face up on the table. "Here it is, about twenty miles above Allentown." The three of them jostled out the door, glad to have someplace to fly, rather than to circle aimlessly over the city for an hour.

When we returned from our flight to York, we found that our friends had just returned from their trip, pale and shaken. The two passengers left rather abruptly, I thought, so we three pilots retired to the Philadelphia Aviation Country Club for some nerve tonic.

"What happened?" I asked the trembling Tri-Pacer pilot, as he sat with his forehead resting in the palm of his left hand, his eyes glassily staring into space like those of a stuffed owl.

Slowly his head swiveled and he looked at me blankly, out of focus.

"You and your games," he said, not without rancor—then swung around and looked out the window.

Bit by bit, the story came out. The first twenty minutes of their flight had been routine, the passengers gaping at the beautiful scenery and the pilot pointing out towns and landmarks. Tempus fugited. The pilot saw, from his watch, that he should be near the airport, although he had not been paying much attention to where he was, so he told the two passengers to look for a grass field with airplanes parked on it; the game of "Where's the airport?" had begun.

Suddenly, one of the eagle-eyed passengers said excitedly, "There are some planes," and pointed down to the right. The pilot's forehead furrowed as he squinted at the chart in his lap. Could that be the airport? It wasn't where the chart said it should be, and there is no airport on the chart where he thought he was. He rolled the plane around and there, sure enough, *was* an airport, so he headed into the wind and landed, rolling up to the several planes tied down at the side of the field.

"Frank," he said, as the nerve medicine took effect, and he began to come unglued, "honest to God, I got the biggest shock of my life! From all sides people converged on us from the woods at the edge of the field, men, women and children—beautiful girls, gorgeous girls— and they didn't have so much as a handkerchief in the group!" He fixed me with a forlorn look. "Playing your game, I landed in a nudist camp!"

He downed some amber fluid and continued: "I didn't know where to look. I didn't know what to say. I was never so embarrassed in my life. Yet they crowded around and were glad to see us. They even wanted us to join them, but we didn't. You know why? One of my passengers was an ordained minister and the other was my boss' son. I'm a wreck. I don't even remember taking off."

We broke out the charts and compared his Commonwealth chart with the New York sectional, issued by Uncle Sam, and saw how the mistake had come about.

The charts were almost alike, except for one detail: On the FAA chart there is an airport named "Sunny Rest" four miles east of the Lehighton strip, a symbol that has been completely eliminated from the state-issued chart because of censorship or something, I suppose. No nudes is good nudes to the Pennsylvania Department of Aeronautics, it seems.

If you are ever in the mood for new fields to conquer, write to Velda Supplee, Sunny Rest Lodge, Route 1, Palmerton, Pa., and get the details. They tell me he is a good guy and welcomes visitors. Personally, I don't think I could take it. I have a low boiling point.

11. Is Flying Dangerous?

A few years ago a short, loud German, name of Adolf, writing a book while ensconced in the local clink, came up with the idea that if he repeated a lie, no matter how big, often enough, everyone would sooner or later believe it to be the gospel truth. Adolf, happily, is no longer with us, but his theory, screwy as it seems, is still pure gold.

Aircraft manufacturers are faced with an enormous problem of sales resistance, mostly because of unwitting and unintended anti-flying propaganda on the part of the newspapers, whose lurid, circulation-building stories have given the lay, or nonflying, public the impression that every aircraft accident results in the death of the majority on board the plane, and that there are a lot of airplane crashes. Both of these ideas are wrong but persistent, for the natural result of this lopsided reporting is to create a towering fear of flying in most people's minds, just as effectively as if the papers were using the technique of Adolf. It seems to me that the aviation industry is never going to sell to a mass market until the scared public is properly informed as to the slight degree of the danger they might expect to face in the air, instead of letting people think of flying as a form of Russian roulette.

The sales technique and approach of the automobile and light-plane manufacturers run almost along the same lines—the emphasis is on horsepower, speed and economy for the men, and comfort and style for the ladies. With the exception of occasional oblique references to turret tops, recessed knobs on the dashboard and safety belts, no one ever talks to a prospective customer along the line that the automobile, which he is looking at with his hand on his wallet, might possibly be involved in a nasty smash.

Despite continual editorializing in the daily newspapers on the subject of automobile accidents in which people are maimed and killed, the average person never really considers the possibility of his becoming a statistic in the casualty reports. It is a matter of mental conditioning; so many of us drive and ride in cars that we feel safe in them. They are a part of our way of life; we take them for granted. But airplanes are misunderstood machines, supported mysteriously by what people still refer to as "the thin air," which is in itself a complete mystery to them. And what people do not understand, they fear.

This is the problem which faces the light-plane manufacturers, and curbs the sale of planes: the reporting of airplane accidents has always been so far overemphasized in the minds of the public that ordinary advertising can't cope with it.

In my hometown papers in the last year, I have seen reports of plane crashes in Los Angeles, Bolivia, England, Egypt and Williamsport; every one of them was prominently located on the front pages, giving the off-hand impression if one read only the headlines, that all of the accidents reported were concentrated, local matters, and I don't have to remark that most people are headline readers.

Is it any wonder, then, that everyone who starts to fly has a gnawing fear lurking in the back of his mind that there is a real danger of the engine stopping or of his having a serious crack-up? I admit that I felt such a fear until I had made my first long cross-country flight with Bob Angeli holding my hand.

So what do most people in the aviation business do? They studiously ignore crack-ups; they never discuss them; they hide them in the closet when company comes, hoping that the subject won't come up. And the worst part of the effect of this ostrich mentality is that it allows the rumor-mongers to win by default, and, like most gossip, the simple facts become distorted beyond all recognition. As a lawyer, I know that there are two sides to every question, but too many people refuse to listen to the whole story. As my wife said to me once in an argument: "It's going to take more than *facts* to convince me I'm wrong!"

The abject fear with which so many people regard private flying and its fancied dangers is something that cannot be analyzed logically, because these people can't usually give any real reasons for being afraid. If it were as dangerous as they profess, no one but lunatics would fly. Yet, it is almost impossible to "get through" to such people; they just keep repeating "It's too dangerous," "It's too dangerous," "It's too dangerous," like a broken record, and refuse to listen.

I have a friend who is a construction engineer, a steel

fabricator. He doesn't think twice about strolling the length of a four-inch-wide beam ten stories in the air, to examine a riveted joint, yet he is afraid of flying—"It's too dangerous!"

Another friend regularly rides to hounds. On different occasions he has fractured his skull, broken his leg and numerous ribs and suffered more bruises being thrown from horses than a peach gets in a super-market, yet he won't go up in an airplane—"It's too dangerous!"

Just how dangerous is flying for a private pilot? After I had flown twenty thousand miles without a scratch, I decided to find out for my own edification how dangerous it really is and was astounded by the results of my investigation—it seems that flying is safer than most anything we do.

First of all, we must realize that "safety" and "danger" are really relative terms. No one is ever absolutely safe, even if he stays in bed twenty-four hours a day and pulls the covers up over his head. Heaven knows we all do things that are dangerous daily as a matter of course —take baths, climb ladders, jaywalk, drive cars too fast, walk down steps without holding on to the banister, overload electric lines, smoke in gasoline stations, and on and on; at the end of the year the insurance companies publish lists of the most dangerous place to be: usually the lists show that most people are injured in their own homes. We know that the annual loss of life from automobile accidents is greater than the loss of life during a war, yet almost everyone engages in driving and considers it a "safe" means of transportation.

Why, then, should people be so afraid of light-plane flying? It is true, however, that the average person will try to draw some comparison between automobiles and airplanes, to create some sort of parallel in his own mind to fill the void of flying knowledge by associating flying with the physical experience of driving a car.

This mental conditioning is almost universal. I can predict that within five minutes after someone learns that I am a private pilot he will ask patronizingly: "What do you do if the engine quits?" Then, having assumed that engine failure is the major hazard of flying, he may be expected to continue in the same vein, drawing the inevitable comparison: "If an automobile engine stops, you get out and fix it."

Or, as the old saying goes, "When your car engine stops, there you are; but when your airplane engine stops, where are you?"

I know how safe aircraft engines are from personal experience, but if I just laugh the question off as silly the questioner usually feels that he has asked me something impossible to answer.

"How long have you been driving a car?" I ask usually evoking the reply that he has been driving for many years.

"How many engine failures have you had on the highway?"

Most people furrow their brows and answer that they never had such an experience, but a few will tell me that they have suffered stoppages from broken rotors or sticking-points in the distributor, or a dead battery because the voltage regulator went on the blink, or a failure of the fuel pump—and then I have my chance to explain how an airplane engine works.

An airplane engine operates independently of the electrical system (battery, generator, voltage regulator) hence a failure of any of these parts will not affect it. The spark is delivered to the cylinders from high intensity spark generators called "magnetos" geared to the crankshaft—and there are two separate ignition systems: two magnetos, two sets of wires, two spark plugs to each cylinder—and the engine will run on either of them. Before take-off the pilot starts the engine with both sets of ignition systems turned on (remember how the ignition switch has a "right-left-both" on it?) and at the end of the runway prior to lifting into the blue he turns off each set of magnetos one at a time to be sure that both are operating all right. Dual ignition gives us two bites at the safety apple. The storage battery in an airplane is used to feed power to the radio, the navigating and landing lights and the self-starter, but if it goes dead the airplane will still fly.

Thus there is no distributor to go sour, no points to stick; the weak links in the internal-combustion engine have been eliminated.

There are sometimes weaknesses in the fuel systems of cars such as failure of the fuel pump, water in the gasoline, or just plain running out of the old go-juice through inattention as most people experience sooner or later in cars.

A pilot worth his salt is very conscious of how much gasoline he has in his tanks, for most of us plan a cross-country flight so as to allow ourselves to arrive at our destination, fly from there to an alternate airport and still have at least a half-hour's worth of the precious fluid when we arrive over the alternate airport.

Water in the gasoline is a condition that may occur as the result of condensation inside partially filled fuel tanks when an airplane stands on the ground for a few days. This condition can for all practical purposes be prevented by filling the tanks to the brim every time the plane lands, thus not allowing any air space inside the tanks, and if the pilot does suspect that there may be some water in the line he can eliminate it by draining a cupful of the gasoline in the drain valve, located at the lowest part of the fuel system. Water, being heavier than gasoline will settle in the valve, and thus flows onto the ground when the pilot, performing his preflight inspection, opens the drain for a few seconds.

An airplane engine has no fuel pump like the ones in cars. Gasoline is fed to the carburetor by gravity in the high-wing models and by air pressure in the low-wing models. If the mechanical pump fails, you can maintain pressure with a hand pump, often called a "wobble pump," until you can find a place to land.

On the instrument panel there are gauges to show the pilot how everything is going: oil-pressure and temperature gauges, cylinder head temperature gauges, manifold pressure gauges, ammeters, a tachometer and, often, a suction gauge. If any of these gauges are not operating in the proper segment, the pilot gets an immediate indication that trouble may be brewing—there aren't many chances of an engine quitting without some advance warning. Visually checking the fuel and oil levels, examining the wiring and fittings, draining the sediment bowl and gas tank sumps would avoid about 90 per cent of the "engine failure" cases.

Assuming that the operators make good preflight checks and take reasonable care of their power plants, are light-plane engines reliable? Let's look at the written record of the one I know best.

My Cessna was flown for the first time on the twenty-first day of September, 1946, powered by a Continental four-cylinder eighty-five-horsepower engine (C-85-12-#23421-6-12).

In its first year, the plane flew all over the East Coast, including a jaunt to Miami and return, almost seventeen thousand miles in all; yet when the engine was one year old, with one hundred and sixty hours on the log, it was checked over and relicensed. The only mechanical "work" required was to clean and gap the spark plugs and to tighten all the engine bolts.

On September 25, 1948, *two* years after it was started for the first time, with two hundred and eighty hours of operation under its belt, the generator brushes were cleaned, and that's all. Thirty thousand miles (based on an average airspeed of one hundred ten miles per hour) and, so far, it had cost three dollars and fifty cents for repairs; and three months later it purred from Wings to Kansas City, Missouri; thence to St. Louis; French Lick, Indiana; and back to Philadelphia, operating as smoothly as a sewing machine.

On this last trip the pilot entered on the log that there was a slight oil loss, and the plane was checked in with the shop, where it was discovered that a "hairline crack" had developed in the oil tank. This was repaired by a simple weld, after the gasoline was drained to avoid fire hazard—cost: one dollar and fifty cents. While the fuel tanks were empty, the opportunity was taken to install a primer-line shield, the carburetor was "de-gunked"; at the same time the airplane's tail wheel was rebushed. The plane was washed, and certified airworthy. Please notice that the engine itself needed nothing in the way of repairs. It was not until June of 1949 that any replacement was made on the C-85. At that time Continental issued a bulletin, M-48-18, to all 140 owners, regarding a new generator drive gear and one was installed, although there had been no malfunction during the three hundred and sixty-one hours of operation.

September 1, 1949, *three* years after its manufacture, at 407 hours on the engine clock, the equivalent of 44,770 miles of flying, the engine was drained, washed down, the plugs gapped, and checked out as perfect for the annual licensing.

In October of 1950, the engine was over *four* years old, with 660 hours (72,600 miles); yet, for the annual relicensing, all that was needed was a new rotor in the right magneto. Cost: about one buck.

At that time the Cessna was doing a lot of night flying to New York and Baltimore, as well as the usual cross-countries all over the East Coast, yet it was not until April of 1953, at the age of *six and one-half years*, that the engine had its first "top" overhaul: the piston rings, rod bearings and valves were replaced and the engine "broken in" again. On the engine clock were 897 hours (98,670 miles) without a hitch in its operation.

All through 1954 the plane was flown without mechanical trouble, and between January 1 and January 10, 1955, flew from Philadelphia to Miami and back, twelve hours each way.

In March of 1955, the logbook shows that the front oil seal was replaced, and the airplane flown from Wings to North Carolina and back. In May of 1955, I became the new owner.

All through the summer of 1955 I commuted daily from Wings to Ocean City, New Jersey, and flew to Boston, Pittsburgh, Mount Pocono, Long Island, and the Eastern Shore of Maryland, and never really heard the C-85 miss a beat.

Recently I flew the 140 from Philadelphia to Hartford, Connecticut, and back in three and a half hours of flying time, using nineteen gallons of gas and one pint of oil. The mag check, prior to take-off at Brainard Field, Hartford, showed a loss of twenty-five rpm on one mag and fifty rpm on the other; a loss of one hundred rpm is permissible. When I landed at Wings, the engine clock read almost nineteen hundred hours—which amounts to almost two hundred ten thousand miles of faultless operation—yet it still ran as smoothly as it had nine long years ago when it first pulled the 140 into the Kansas sky.

Now, I am the typical modern American. When a larger size television screen comes on the market, my old one is quickly traded in, and when my automobile has 50,000 miles on its speedometer, I look upon it as an antique (and by that time it seems that most cars are acting like antiques). Upon this basis of comparison, the safety, reliability and consistent operation of modern light-plane engines stand out as a monument to the manufacturer. The person who asks condescendingly, "What do you do if the engine stops?" as if it is *sure* to happen, obviously doesn't realize the mechanical marvels that power our airplanes.

Suppose an airplane is flying two thousand feet high at normal cruise, and the engine stops. Does the plane drop like a bucket of sand? Do the wings fall off? Does it go into a tail spin? It does not.

By virtue of an engine failure, a plane is changed into a glider, maintaining its lift during a gradual descent;—

it still flies, just the way it does on every landing approach and, as long as the pilot maintains enough airspeed to keep the lift in the wings and control the plane, he is in no immediate danger. The problem before him is to find a place to put it down and then to get into that space with flying control.

Remember that to slow the plane down, he pulls the wheel back, and speeds up by pushing it forward. If the pilot pulls too far back, so that the nose stays high, the plane will lose too much of its flying speed and drain off its lift in a stall, and that is where the danger lies—in a low altitude stall with, perhaps, a spin. As long as the pilot keeps the nose down in a glide at a proper maneuvering speed, he will be able to pick a spot on which to land, even though it may not be a perfect landing field, and accident reports show that if he keeps his head he will be able to land without personal injury.

Suppose you are "letting down" from a five-thousand-foot cruising altitude, spiraling lazily to the airport far below with the engine idling nicely. As you enter the pattern, you give her some juice, and the engine coughs and quits. No strain; just remember to hold the nose down enough to keep the airplane flying—even though the first reaction is to haul back on the wheel—and complete the landing at the airport.

Why might this type of "engine failure" happen? Usually it is for one of two reasons, both avoidable: what fliers refer to as "loading up" or the formation of "carburetor ice."

"Loading up" is a condition that sometimes occurs when an engine idles for a long time, so that a "rich" mixture of fuel in relation to air is sucked into and is swirling around in the intake manifold and cylinder:

then, when the pilot opens the throttle, the mixture is still further enriched, so that the gasoline-to-air ratio is not correct for combustion; it has the same effect as pulling the choke all the way out on your hot automobile engine—when the gas won't burn, the engine stops, from "choking out." So, during a let-down and approach, you keep the "jugs" clear by occasionally opening the throttle for a few seconds, "giving it a burst to clear the plugs." If you don't do this and the engine stops, is it "engine failure" or is it "pilot failure"?

Carburetor icing may occur any time, even on a hot summer day, where there is no moisture visible in the air, for our atmosphere has certain physical properties, such as absorbing moisture in suspension, warming up when compressed (as in a tire pump), and cooling rapidly when rarefied suddenly. You may recall the old refrigeration principle of an expansion valve that allows compressed gas to expand in a coil immersed in water, thus absorbing heat, thereby transforming the water into ice.

The carburetor of a plane's engine contains the niftiest little "expansion valve" you ever saw. The air is forced into an intake port through a constriction called a "venturi" in the pipe thence through a small hole, at which time the air is compressed and heated, then, once through the little hole, it is introduced into a larger chamber and allowed to expand, at which time the air becomes suddenly very cold, sometimes dropping forty or fifty degrees in a thousandth of a second. If there is moisture in the air, it will often be affected by this sudden drop in temperature, and right there, in the throat of the venturi, develops a coat of rime ice which makes the hole smaller. Now, the venturi's purpose is to increase the speed of the air through the carburetor and to vaporize the gasoline but, if the hole gets too small, the air and/or the gasoline can't get through to the cylinders and the engine stops. So, the pilot has a control on the panel to introduce heat into the carburetor so the ice won't form—or will melt off if there is any—and that's why we go through the routine of pulling on the carburetor heat when we are going to change throttle settings. Due to the velocity of the air through the venturi at cruising speed, ice seldom forms, but when the engine is idling it sometimes builds up pretty fast, so my motto is simply, "When in doubt, pull on the carb heat." I've never had any trouble yet.

Suppose, now, that you are taking off, and the engine sputters and dies. Obviously, this is the stickiest kind of failure, because you are at a low altitude, your airspeed is slow, and you already have your nose high. The instructors tell us that the first thing to do is get the nose down to keep flying speed, and *land straight ahead*. Most people who have engine failures on take-off get hurt trying to make it back to the field, which is a natural inclination. But at slow speed, trying to turn often results in a stalling out of the inside wing and down they go.

It seems that the only kind of crash from which few people escape with a whole skin is the straight-down type; a spin or spiral dive close to the earth is about the same as driving a car off a cliff, but on the other hand if one keeps his airspeed and hence his control of the plane, he can get away with almost anything, from hitting a fence to landing in a tree, with only a bent airplane to show for it.

When I started doing research for this chapter, I was

gratified to find that after going through hundreds of accident reports from all parts of the country I had not come across a single fatality; and there were only two serious injuries.

Since the "engine failure" cases seem to be uppermost on everyone's mind, I picked up the first ten reports from the 1954 card files at random and copied down the essential facts of the reports; let's look at some notes taken from official Pennsylvania accident reports of cases where the engine reportedly "failed."

Case No. 1. Pilot flying Navion for the first time solo filled tanks on cross-country flight, became lost and ran out of gas. Landed in wheat field, ran into a small woods along side. No one hurt. (There were still five gallons of gas in the tanks, but pilot did not know how to turn on auxiliary tank).
Conclusion: Pilot failure; didn't know his airplane.

Case No. 2. Pilot flying Stinson 105 had engine quit at seventy-five feet on take-off. Tanks were empty. Electric fuel gauge showed each tank half full. Pilot stalled into a hill and smashed landing gear. No personal injuries.
Conclusion: Pilot failure; no preflight check.

Case No. 3. Pilot topped one tank and took off on the other, almost empty, in a Piper Pacer. While cruising, engine stopped, and he headed for a field, which he undershot, going through some trees, bounced on the landing gear, which collapsed, and went over on his back. No personal injuries, except for a fractured ego.

Conclusion: Pilot failure; tried to fly on empty tank.

Case No. 4.   Pilot making a long let-down used carburetor heat but didn't use throttle. Upon undershooting the approach, he advanced the throttle, but the engine would not pick up. He hit a pole, wrapped up the airplane, total loss. No personal injuries.

Conclusion: Pilot failure, in not jazzing the engine on the way down.

Case No. 5.   Pilot landing, on final approach, had engine quit, landed against a stone fence five hundred feet short of the runway, and wrecked Cessna 140. Left tank was empty —right tank full. Selector was on left tank. No injuries.

Conclusion: Pilot failure.

Case No. 6.   Pilot had Piper engine develop extreme roughness and loss of power on take-off so that he could barely hold altitude. He prayed his way into the pattern, and on final the roughness became very loud and the engine stopped. He landed short of airport on highway and wiped out the landing gear. Inspection disclosed a "seized cylinder." No one hurt.

Conclusion: Engine failure.

Case No. 7.   Pilot noticed extreme vibration on the take-off run in Seabee, chopped throttle fifty feet in the air, turned left and landed hard on the edge of the airport with gear partially up. Prop blade flew off. Pilot seriously injured.

Conclusion: Prop failure, plus pilot failure —tried to turn back to field, instead of landing straight ahead.

Case No. 8. Pilot of Luscombe on local flight had engine quit at eight hundred feet. Landed hard in pasture, hitting tree and wrecking plane. Pilot and passenger slightly hurt. Ran out of gas, despite operating fuel gauges.

Conclusion: Pilot failure, inattention.

Case No. 9. Pilot taking off in J-3 shut off the gas selector valve instead of carburetor heat. Gear wiped out. Pilot unhurt.

Conclusion: Pilot failure.

Case No. 10. Pilot on cross-country when engine stopped, made forced landing in woods. Plane wrecked. Pilot unhurt. Not watching gas gauges, plus leaking carburetor drain responsible for running out of gas.

Conclusion: Pilot failure.

One actual "Engine Failure" out of ten reported ones.

And so it goes, time and time again—the pilot goofs, the plane is wrecked, the occupants get out with a shaking up, and the newspapers say "engine failure causes crash."

Let me not kid you; I am no paragon of virtue in this "stupidity derby," but I learned the hard way that the pilot can trust only himself to make the inspection of the plane before *every* flight.

My baptism came one day when I stopped in at a strange field to gas up and get a cup of coffee. I left the *Legal Eagle* at the gas pits to have the tanks topped while I went in to get my java, and when I got back in the plane a few minutes later I started the engine and taxied over to the end of the strip, preparing for take-off. As I swung around to look for landing planes in the pattern, the engine gave one cough and stopped, dead as a mackerel. I was jolted out of my daydreaming pronto and began to look around the cabin, and there was my fuel selector at "Off." Usually I leave my gas tank selector valve at the "On" position for my left tank, but the line boy had moved it to "Off" when he filled the tanks, and I had not run through my preflight check as I had been taught to do. That's something I will never forget again. But it was not the fault of the engine; just another example of "pilot failure," like all but one of the cases I have cited.

I have concluded that if you treat 'em right, light-plane engines, props and mounts are dependable and trouble-free, and that light-plane pilots do not have to have a pact with Fate to fly with safety.

But don't take my word for it. The National Safety Council recently announced that their studies show that flying in general (which does not include commercial airlines) is approximately *five times safer* than traveling by automobile.

The results of my study of aircraft accidents had begun to fascinate my legally trained brain; what, besides "pilot-failure-type engine failures" is the pattern of aircraft accidents?

I got together with Frank Mayock, the general manager of Wings Field, and we sat for two hours in the

Philadelphia Aviation Country Club, watching hundreds of take-offs and landings through the picture window, talking over light-plane accidents and repairs.

Frank smoked his black pipe and riffled through a pile of papers, going back for years over the records of Wings Field accident reports and repair schedules from the shops.

"How long has this airfield been in operation?" I asked, as a DC-3 settled onto the runway.

"Twenty-seven years," answered the large red-head, almost asphyxiating me with a cloud of smoke from the Old Burlap he was smoking.

"How many fatal accidents have you had here?" I asked, poising a pencil over a large clean yellow pad.

Frank's eyes took on a troubled look, like those of a bloodhound who has lost his last scent.

"Well, I've been here since the war and don't remember any," he said, as if apologizing for the lack of gore on the premises.

"No accidents at all?" I asked.

"Well," he answered with a shrug, "once in a while someone will run into a runway light or another taxiing airplane, or will bend a prop or smash up a landing gear and wing tip on a lousy landing without getting hurt himself. But in twenty-seven years we haven't had a fatality on this field."

So I began to set up one hundred accident reports culled from the Commonwealth of Pennsylvania Department of Aeronautics and the AOPA—reports picked at random which should be fairly representative of the kinds of accidents that happen all over the country.

When I got the reports straightened out and sorted

according to the type of flight activity engaged in at the time of the crash I found that I had six accidents that occurred while taxiing, nine on take-offs, thirty-three while landing, thirty-six caused by flying in conditions of very reduced visibility where the pilots were not instrument-rated, five attributed to buzzing (showing off close to the ground against regulations) and eleven miscellaneous accidents which included four lost pilots who ran out of gas (two at night) and made forced landings, one plane that reportedly "blew up," one passenger that fell out of the plane during a loop (loops are also against regulations) and one guy that ran into a mountain in the fog. Incidentally, there was not a fire in the bunch.

Time after time the weather accidents said something like this: "Tail pointing upwards and general condition of wreckage indicates impact with the ground at a steep nose-down attitude and high speed. Probably a spiral dive or spin out of weather. Pilot was licensed for flying only under visual conditions."

Well, there it is. The killer in aviation is violating rules of common sense and of the Federal Aviation Administration. If a pilot takes a chance by showing off at low altitude or by trying to fly on instruments when he is not qualified, the odds are very much against his collecting Social Security. A low altitude stall and spin, from three hundred feet, for instance, is about the same as driving a car off the top of a thirty-story building. And the spiral dive from an altitude of several thousand feet usually causes the plane to shed its wings on the way down, so the smash is even harder—not that it makes a great deal of difference to the occupants.

But if you follow the FAA Regulations to the letter—don't fly in bad weather, don't buzz, don't take a chance, ever—flying is an extremely safe pastime.

Many nonfliers have the idea from newspaper stories that the sky around big cities is literally black with airplanes, all hurtling through space like so many winged bullets, and that there is a terrible danger of mid-air collision. This is another hazard that is magnified out of all proportion as far as a-hundred-and-twenty-mph planes are concerned. I have flown over New York, Washington, Chicago, Miami and Philadelphia when the air traffic was considered heavy, yet have never been nearer than two miles to another plane, until I got near an airport or into a landing pattern (then a pilot is really safer from collision than at any other time, because he is alert, looking around for other planes; and at big airports he is in direct radio contact with the tower, the "traffic policeman" for the field, who separates and spaces the planes and brings them in individually while keeping all the others out of the way).

There are also certain regulations, governing the altitudes at which you must fly on different headings on cross-countries. As Bob Angeli told me: "It's all in the book or on the back of the charts."

What about the six-hundred mph jets? First of all they usually fly at thirty to fifty thousand feet (except while in take-off or landing pattern) far above us light-plane pilots—and so do airliners.

Furthermore, I want to make it clear again for the umpteenth time that as a private pilot I fly only when the weather is good enough to see for miles, and I keep my head on a swivel all the time. Not only is this required by law of every pilot, but no cautious person is going to fly when he can't see where he is going and what else is in the air around him—law or no law. The guy who takes a chance on flying through fog has only himself to blame if he suddenly finds that the fog is full of rocks, structural steel or another airplane.

On a gorgeous fall afternoon, my partner and I were returning from a business trip from Boston to Philadelphia in the 140. At six thousand feet over Meriden, Connecticut, we could see the blue water of the Atlantic Ocean eighty miles away to our left, beyong Long Island, and before us the countryside spread in soft folds and ripples like a plush green carpet.

Tom was flying at the time, while I listened to the Cornell-Princeton football game on the headphones. He nudged me with his elbow and I slid the right phone up on the side of my head, above my ear.

"Call Bridgeport Tower," he said, "and get the winds aloft over New York City."

I put my cigarette in the ashtray on the left door, slid the right phone back over my ear and spun the receiver to the Bridgeport frequency, 203 kilocycles. As I reached for the mike with my left hand, my elbow unlatched the window and it opened with a snap. Instantly a cold gale swirled around the little cabin. Maps, flight plans and memoranda began blowing in all directions, and I saw, out of the corner of my eye, a shower of sparks as my cigarette tumbled end over end in the vortex, right over the back of the seat. I couldn't see whether the lighted tip had blown out the window or inside, where it might be smoldering in the luggage compartment's thick carpeting. All I could think of was "fire in the air."

Quickly I unsnapped my safety belt and knelt on my

seat facing backwards, scrambling with both hands in the baggage section.

Tom yelled at me, "Whaddya doing?"

I didn't answer; I was too busy.

"What's the matter?" he hollered again.

I looked at him for a full second. "I think we're on fire," I answered, and he looked like Sambo the night the owl screeched in the cemetery.

I finally found the butt, minus tip. No fire. Scared us, though.

No, the real hazards of flying are not the ones that can be compared with the hazards of driving automobiles, and they are not the ones that almost every nonflier thinks they are, either: engine failures are almost unheard of—real engine failures, that is—tail spins are nothing to fear, and mid-air collisions don't happen to a careful pilot who looks where he is going.

The danger in flying goes right back to the technical and psychological qualifications of the pilot. The old saying that the most critical part of an airplane, the part that fails most often and is responsible for nearly all airplane accidents is "the nut that holds the wheel."

The pilot who dozes on the job, who assumes that he is safe simply because the laws of probability make a collision possible, though a long, long shot in the vastness of the sky—the pilot who blithely flies along in the teeth of a weather front until he finally blunders into a flight condition that is beyond his flying ability, like plunging into instrument conditions when he is not an instrument pilot, or flying an airplane with which he is not completely familiar—he is the culprit.

Proper instruction from the outset, and thereafter periodic check flights with your instructor, is the answer to most of these problems. After you have the "feel" of your airplane, and have developed a pattern of safe habits, you avoid most aerial traps that cause accidents. Don't be afraid or ashamed to ask for a check ride once in a while to smooth out rough spots that may have developed in your technique. There is no reason why a week-end pilot can't be just as proficient as a commerical pilot. And you have an advantage now; you have a glimmering of the thing that no laymen and few pilots realize: that airplane accidents fall into a pattern which can be predicted by the experts on the basis of past experience and, knowing the real hazards, you can avoid them. The most important thing to remember is that the danger lies in trying to fly an airplane with the wheel too far back; that bad technique produces more fatal accidents than anything, and if the pilot has been well trained he will be able to avoid this hazard. Once you know what the problem is, you can lick it.

So what is a fair conclusion as to the danger of flying?

In the sense that you can be hurt, flying is dangerous —the same as driving a car is dangerous or climbing a stool to replace a light bulb or playing golf on a public links or going hunting with a high-powered rifle.

But, so help me, if you don't monkey with the weather, don't buzz, know your airplane, learn good flying technique, and thus avoid most of the pitfalls of the air, it seems crystal clear that, relatively speaking, flying is a lot safer than any of these other activities, and a lot more fun than staying in bed with the covers pulled over your head.

12. Wheels, Keels and Deals

Somewhere recently I read a statement to the effect that there is no longer any middle class in America and that that is what is wrong with us, among other things. I think the article was written by an Englishman. Of course, he was dead wrong in his conclusion, because he started from a false assumption. In England, you see, they don't pretend to be democratic; they have pretty well defined social strata, and the average person apparently is happy with his position in life and doesn't cultivate an ulcer crop just to show that he is as good as Lord Windershmere.

This happy condition of social equilibrium is not the case in the United States of North America. No sir. *We* are "democratic." No one is better than anyone else, here. Are we snobs who make a person's wealth the sole criterion of his worth? You're darn right we are! Americans are snobs of the worst type, although we profess not to be, and deride our British friends for being so class-conscious; no one in the middle class of the United States can escape the result of our snob-mentality. Rather than be satisfied to live at our income level, we climb to the next highest level to show the rich man that we are as good as he is. The symptoms of the snob cholera are easy to recognize: you cringe when you enter a parking lot and find that your Ford is conspicuous in a yard full of Continentals, Cadillacs and Jaguars; your wife drops out of the ladies' bridge because everyone has a mink muff but her; you hesitate to invite a recently met nice couple to your home for an evening because you know that they have a larger house than yours. So you thereupon sally forth and draw on the exchequer for a Mercedes, a mink or a mansion. "Keeping up with the Joneses" is a recognized type of dementia Americana wherein we spend money we can't afford to buy things we don't need to impress people that don't matter. This is known as "ulcer economy"; and that's what has happened to our middle class: it's hiding from the sheriff and the finance company.

It depresses me and is a sad commentary upon our mentality that, despite our professed democratic way of life, certain products are openly merchandised by advertising campaigns stressing their snob appeal; that types of automobiles are sold on the premise that the owner —be he a judge or a janitor—thereby acquires prestige in the community, even though in the final analysis a ten-thousand-dollar car won't do anything better, in terms of transportation, than a three- or four-thousand-dollar one, and that the guy driving the prestige car may have a criminal record as long as your arm.

My frau warns me that, since I have my own airplane and am happy, I am becoming a "snob snob"; that I am too intolerant of the faker who, at a party, loudly makes it known that he has recently acquired a new super-chromed Wombat-Twelve that is guaranteed to go 140 mph in second gear and will change its own tires when the driver presses a button on the dash; but the truth of the matter is that it is she who usually deals the crusher to the braggart where it hurts him the most— right smack in the center of his ego.

"Oh, that Frank," she will say to no one in particular, just at the opportune moment when the bore stops to get his breath, "he has wall-to-wall carpeting in his airplane, even in the luggage compartment." This has a pronounced double-barreled effect on the blowhard, first by taking all the wind out of his sails and, secondly, by tossing the conversational ball to me the instant he fumbles it.

"*You* have an *airplane?*" some girl will almost invariably gush, and I will studiously flick some imaginary lint from my lapel and, underplaying the part to the utmost, shyly admit that, yes, I have one. The attention recently given the car-snob fastens on me; instantly I have become a big man; I have become suddenly promoted from the "poor but honest lawyer" category in everyone's mind, and am looked upon as an entrepreneur, a financier and a man to be reckoned with and respected. In short, I, as the owner of a $1500 airplane, have completely eclipsed the owner of a $15,000 Juggernaut who, it is to be hoped, will promptly leave the party and throw himself prone before a speeding car on the nearest highway. Preferably a Wombat-Twelve.

Of course, I realize that the fickle admirers don't know the actual cost of my 140. They think, like most people, that it set me back $20,000, and I don't enlighten them right away.

But when the party has shaken down to the few bitterenders who I know are good guys, and the men, as a group, have left the women alone to talk about children and have moved the bar operations into the kitchen, I let them know the truth about the cost of flying, and pursed lips and squinted eyes show me that my message is getting across. Flying, as I do it, is not expensive, yet owning a plane is far more of a "prestige" factor than owning any car.

Private flying, just like boating, automobiling, golfing or playing the ponies, can put you in the poorhouse if you overextend yourself. Few of us can afford either a fifty-foot twin-screw cruiser, a double Nassau or a Beechcraft Bonanza as pure luxuries; but anyone who can operate a twenty-five-horsepower outboard cruiser can afford to run a light plane that will cruise over a hundred mph with a range of four hundred miles, and have radio equipment, too!

Just as I was ignorant before I jumped into flying two years ago, most people are cowed by their misapprehensions about light-plane flying, not only as to the difficulty, or lack of it, in learning to fly, and of the hazards involved, but also as to the expense of buying and operating a private plane.

"It's a rich man's hobby," they say. "I couldn't afford it." I often wonder why someone in the business hasn't set them straight before this. Look: the Research Institute of America, which keeps a close check on our buying habit patterns, has recently released figures to show that, within the next ten years, the "expensive" leisure-time sports like boating, which grew in ownership from 1945 to 1970 to ten million boats, should double every ten years and that currently "Sunday sailors," as the trade calls them, are spending one billion dollars a year for pleasure craft and supplies.

Many of my airplane-expense-fearing friends already have boats at the seashore or on the lakes ranging from twelve-foot outboards to sixty-foot cabin cruisers, upon which they lavish money, love, money, affection, money, time—and money—all for a period of at most three or four months each year.

What do they do with these boats? During June, July and August they fish once or twice a week, tow water skiers, ride around as fast as they can, do some exploring around the bays, lakes or canals, and return to their dock.

Understand I am not knocking this as fun, but I in-nire of my boating friends, "How about those months om September to the following June, when the boat is p on dry land far from the water, and just waiting for he coming spring when it will be scraped, caulked, sanded, painted and otherwise fussed with?" For those months ye owner must seek solace in his memories, his picture album and the mating call of the Brooklyn Dodger fan—"Wait till next year!"

Come wintertime I can relate at a social gathering that that day I have been to Laconia or Roaring Branch, and all ears perk up with interest at the tale; but if I suggest that some of my boating friends should take up flying, they all say, "Not for me, I can't afford it." The speaker may have a $3500 Chris-Craft but he says he can't "afford" to run a plane; and he means it—only because he doesn't realize how cheap a plane is to own and operate. As the French say, "It is to laugh."

Why do people spend so much money on boats, with their restricted utility both as to the time they are usable and as to the distance they can cover, yet hold back from engaging in the sport of flying, a year-round proposition of enormous range? It seems to me that there are several reasons: when they think of flying, they usually think only of new planes, which admittedly are too expensive for the average guy to use purely for putzing around; and they don't trust second-hand planes any more than they trust most second-hand cars. There is no logical comparison between buying used cars and used airplanes; where cars are mechanical jig-saw puzzles, as complicated as a woman and worn out generally after five years, airplanes are simple in their structure and, except for the engine, control cables, wheels and fabric, there is really nothing that will wear out, no matter how much it is used, assuming no one has ever tried to fly it through a brick wall. The conclusion is that inspection of these parts frequently and replacment of them, if necessary, keeps a plane in tip-top shape, as good as new.

Furthermore, people are "boat-conditioned" by relentless advertising campaigns: the boat companies are out to build up a large low-cost market because they know from past experience that a man who has even a small boat is going to buy a larger one as soon as he can and, in this aspect particularly, we can see that there is a tremendous difference between the sales approach of boat manufacturers and those who make airplanes. While the Elco Boat Company sells one $50,000 cruiser-type yacht, it markets hundreds of Do-It-Yourself "kit-boats," selling for less than one thousand dollars, the idea being to reach a volume market to get people into some kind of a boat.

On the other hand, the Piper Aircraft Company sells one $50,000 Twin-Comanche Apache to four or five $15,000 Cherokees, both of which are obviously priced way above the average Joe's ability to pay. As a result the plane people must try to sell their products to the business and utility market—to businessmen, farmers, prospectors and surveyors, and forget the volume market composed of those who could afford to pay two or three grand for a plane as a hobby, pure and simple.

This situation has not gone unnoticed. Some designers have designed and are selling "kit-type" one- and two-place airplanes to be assembled by the buyer, cruising over eighty-five to 200 mph and some of them costing less than a thousand dollars, yet in every sense high performance airplanes despite their tiny size. The only drawback to kit planes is that there are a lot of people like myself who can't build anything with their hands and who will shy away especially quickly from building anything upon which their safety would depend. I once built my wife a storage closet, and the very first time she closed the door the shelves collapsed and I had to clean the mess up, so I know I am not going to try to build me an airplane, although there are a lot of people who can, and I hope will, buy kits, and "roll-their-own." Check the Experimental Aircraft Association, 11311 West Forest Home Avenue, Franklin, Wisconsin for details.

Aside from the Stits Aircraft Company, no other current manufacturer is even attempting to reach us "weekenders"; except for dusting and spraying models, none of them seem to make two-place light planes any more, only four-place "business" planes.

This is by no means meant to be a criticism of the position taken by the airplane manufacturers; it is a condition that exists in the new plane market, resulting from the trend of our national economy. Twenty years ago, pork chops were thirty cents a pound; ten thousand dol-

lars a year was a top executive's salary, and cars sold for
five hundred dollars. Ten years ago, the spiral of inflation was in full swing and, as the national income went
up, the cost of living followed it; the income tax structure was changed by the Congress to raise money for the
Government, siphoning off a lot of personal income.
For these and many other reasons, the prices of new
cars and new planes have gone up tremendously in the
last ten years, but then so has the quality of the cars and
the planes. A new four-place Cherokee will set you back
about eighteen G's, where ten years ago the same type of
plane, slower maybe, and not so high-powered, would
have cost four or five thousand dollars. As soon as the
average person sees the price tag on a new plane, he
turns around and walks right out of the flying game; yet
for some reason no manufacturer has yet stressed to the
public that there is an advantage to the "business-
market" trend as far as the sportsman-pilot is concerned, and then followed-up his interest: although a
man cannot afford, as an individual, to lay out eight
thousand dollars for a new plane, active corporations
and businesses can, and the Federal Corporate Income
Tax structure, allowing a useful tax life of five years for
"write-offs," has produced a used-plane market, enabling
the individual to get into flying about as cheaply as he
can get into boating. As far as the feared initial expense
is concerned, there are thousands of used planes for sale
right now for less than the cost of an outboard cruiser
and its motor.

If a plane has been used as a "commercial carrier,"
that is, for charter work or for instruction, it has been
subject to particularly strict regulations governing inspection, repairs and relicensing. It is, therefore, not

imprudent to purchase such a "used" plane, provided it has recently been inspected and relicensed (which, incidentally, can be done only by an FAA certified mechanic who has gone through a long course of training, and then been tested by Uncle Sam). You can be sure in buying such a used plane that the crankcase won't be stuffed with sawdust, or that an engine crack has not been "repaired" with putty. A used airplane with a new license is often in better shape, mechanically, than a new airplane just out of the factory; all the "bugs" have been worked out of it.

There must be some reason why the airplane manufacturers haven't gone into "trade-in" merchandising in which they would take used planes in trade for new ones, and sell the used planes advertised as "warranted" or properly "checked" by their own factory-trained mechanics, much the same as automobile manufacturers do; by so doing, they could get a lot of people into flying cheaply and, like the boat sellers, they would build pilots and purchasers for the future. I am not a merchandiser, but it seems to me that they are missing a bet here someplace.

Suppose you do buy a new plane for $1750? What other expenses can you expect to face after the initial outlay? Aside from medical expenses when your wife finds out, I mean.

Except for the cost of learning to fly, operating expenses are not much different from those involved in operating a Ford car or an outboard cruiser and, if you own your plane, even the cost of learning to fly and getting your private license is ridiculously low. If you have to rent a plane, the cost of learning can be pretty steep and, for that reason, I advise everyone to buy, as I did, and get a lot of time on the logbook in his own plane.

The FAA requires that, in order to be rated as a private pilot, you must log a minimum of forty hours from an approved school including seventeen hours of dual instruction and eighteen hours of solo under the orders of your instructor. At the rate of $17 an hour for the airplane (Cessna 150) rental, and $5.00 on top of that for the instructor's time, plus $10.00 for the FAA flight test, it costs about $750 to get your "ticket"; and then you must still shell out every time you want to fly—if you can find a plane available, which is sometimes impossible in nice weather. When you fly larger airplanes, the rental costs go up. I rent Cessna 150's for $20 an hour and Bonanzas for $25 at Wings; that is about the going rate for these planes, and neither flying nor taxi-riding is fun when you keep thinking of that meter ticking away.

I learned to fly in my own plane and my out-of-pocket expenses (after the initial outlay of $1500) were a mere $60 for the instructor and $89 for gas and oil, or a total of $156, including the flight test fee—and I had the plane available any time I wanted it for as long as I wanted to fly it. There is nothing sadder to see than the fellow who sweats out his instruction a half hour at a time; then, once he has his license, can get aloft only once every month for an hour or two. That poor guy can never learn to be proficient at the art of flying since he never goes anywhere except on local flights for an hour or two at the most. So you can see why I am ownership-minded and think it is cheaper in the long run to buy a plane, strange as it may have seemed at first.

Let's look at my operating cost records for one year: I flew my 140 two hundred hours at a cruise of one hundred ten to one hundred fifteen mph airspeed—roughly twenty-two thousand miles. Burning five gallons of gas per hour, I used one thousand gallons, plus forty quarts of oil, for a total cost of almost $400.

Since the plane has fabric-covered wings, I hangar it in the wintertime, although it sits outside all summer (and has ridden out three hurricanes, to boot); the tie-down and hangar costs averaged $15 a month and the total costs came to $190, according to the logbook.

The annual relicensing costs $25 and the repairs have never exceeded $75 a year for new sparkplugs, inspections and such. Six hundred sixty dollars. Is that too expensive? Let me tell you, my friends, it is cheap. Six hundred sixty dollars is a trifle more than twelve dollars a week—less than I used to drink at bars to show how successful I was.

Six hundred sixty dollars of expense to cover twenty thousand miles comes out to three and one-third cents a mile, or one and two-third cents per seat-mile for my out-of-pocket expenses, not counting the original cost of the plane or "depreciation."

Suppose I had rented a plane to do that kind of flying. A Cherokee would have cost me $3600 and, after shelling out the dineros, all I would have had is a few memories and numbers in my logbook. Also a cleaver in my skull from friend wife.

And here comes the clincher: the most surprising and little-known fact about light-plane flying is that you can buy a used plane for less than the price of a used car, although it is in excellent shape, fly it for two years, keeping it in good condition, and then sell it for approximately the same price you paid for it!

Of course, the expense of flying, like the expense of boating, depends on whether you use the craft purely for pleasure or partly for business or charter; whether you keep it on your own landing strip or must rent parking space for it; whether you own it individually or with others. But the more you fly, the less it costs per mile, since the fixed costs are thereby stretched over a great deal more use of the plane.

"Where do you find used planes?" people ask me regularly, and seem surprised when I tell them that there are aircraft brokers that operate like yacht brokers, and that there are trade papers subscribed to by thousands of people looking for used planes. (See the appendix for a list.)

"The plane I could afford wouldn't be worth a whistle," say the doubters; then I start to tell them about the utility of the "under $2000 class" planes, the Luscombes, Aeroncas, Cessna 120's and 140's, Ercoupes and Swifts. Are they toys, or puddle jumpers, suitable only for flying around the home airport? After I relate how I have flown my 140 everywhere from Boston to Miami and Niagara Falls to Kansas City, they know that they are not toys. I can cite other examples:

Not long ago, a young Swiss visitor rented a Cessna 120 at Wings and flew to the West Coast, as a tourist wanting to see America. The round trip covered fifty-four hundred miles, cost eight hundred and ten dollars, and took ten days of flying, during which he used three hundred and thirty-one gallons of gas and eleven and one-half quarts of oil, averaging ninety-five and nine-tenths miles an hour ground speed. The trip cost him fifteen cents per mile, including all expenses. Can you drive your car on such a trip that cheaply? Or as safely? Can you see as much as he saw?

I know of two college students who left Seattle, Washington, in their own Luscombe float plane and flew all the way around the United States in ninety flying hours, flying only five and a half hours a day. The total flying costs for gas and oil were one hundred and sixty-two dollars for a vacation I'm sure they will never forget. Doesn't that give you the itch?

Let's assume you decide to buy a plane in which to get your private ticket; what is the best type of plane to take your student training in? I strongly recommend that you buy the plane you want to use for your fun-flying later on, even if it is a Bonanza, and learn in that. I am in the minority in so advising, for there is an often-expressed theory that the best type of a plane in which to take basic training is one having a very slow landing speed, and after mastering that plane, you can "step up" into bigger, faster, heavier equipment.

People around airports refer to the old tried and true sixty-five-horsepower Piper J-3 Cub as being a "forgiving" airplane, meaning that the student pilot can make mistakes and get away with them because the airplane is so slow that he has lots of time in which to make corrections. Maybe this is true but, as far as I am concerned, the theory is a lot of hooey.

When I was searching through accident files, I saw reports of J-3's being hung in trees, on wires, ground-looped and pancaked, and concluded that even if a plane lands at five miles an hour the pilot's safety still depends on his exercise of good judgment and, if he has none, the airplane's forgiving characteristic won't save him forever.

Don't listen to all the idle chatter you may hear about different types of airplanes. For instance, the Cessna 140 apparently has a reputation among some "ten-hour-aces" of being tricky to fly—a little "warm," a "floater" which tips over easily, and all sorts of hogwash that tends to scare new and impressionable student pilots. Fortunately, I never heard those stories until I had over a hundred hours in my 140, so I never knew all the "faults" of the plane. I just started cold and learned how to fly it and, in a short time, I got so that I would fly my 140 anywhere at the drop of a hat—and I dropped the hat.

I suppose it is mostly a feeling of confidence in your instructor when you reduce it to its lowest denominator; I honestly think that Bob Angeli could have started me off in a Swift or a Bonanza, both of which are fast planes. Impossible? Not at all—Andy Andreotti of El Centro, California, took twelve hours of instruction in a Tri-Pacer, then bought a twin-engine Piper Apache and got his private license in that, and had a multi-engine rating before he had one for single engines!

So, I repeat, get an Aeronca, a Cessna, a Piper or Swift, and learn to fly in it; remember that you can always sell it later when you want to grow into a larger plane for your fun and frolic.

If you don't feel that you can buy a plane by yourself, there are many ways of sharing expense by spreading the original investment with some friends, or else you can look around to see if there is a flying club in your vicinity composed of a group of fellows who have joined together in a syndicate or club and will sell shares in a plane. It's a cheap way to fly, whether the club owns a 140 or a Bonanza.

A consulting engineer friend (and client) of mine used to fly a Luscombe 85 (very similar in performance to the Cessna 140) all over the East, both for pleasure and on business; but he found that as his family and business grew, the two-place Luscombe was inadequate for his needs, since very often he wanted to take the family for a visit to the in-laws or take two or three other men with him on business trips.

Being an energetic and ingenious guy, he soon located the plane he wanted—a gorgeous, used, Cessna 170 B, with all sorts of radio, unhappily priced above his means at the time, at $5800. Undaunted, he scouted around to see if there were any people with the same problem he had and, within a week convinced not one, but three flying friends, all of whom did a great deal of flying in their own small planes, that he had the answer to their common problem: syndicate ownership. At a party, while the ladies were otherwise engaged, the five of us got to kicking the thing around. They agreed to form a syndicate to buy the 170, provided I could devise a feasible plan for their equal use of the plane.

Until the dawn's early light, we sat working one up: first, they agreed that the purchase price was to be split evenly four ways, coming to fourteen hundred and fifty dollars apiece for the initial outlay, which would be more than covered by the sales of their old planes. Using a grease pencil freely on the unfinished walls of Hugh's new game room, we set up a set of operating terms and conditions that were later signed by all the conspirators. One drawback had immediately become obvious: since there were to be several owners, no one of them could just go out to the field and fly on a whim without giving any consideration to the possible plans of his partners, for this leads to hypertension, ulcers and broken noses, if overdone.

To avoid trouble on this, we decided to set up a reservation book, to be kept by Hugh who should act as a combined "reservation clerk" and timekeeper; his approval was to be an absolute requirement before the plane could be used and he would maintain a special docket for the purpose of showing who flew it most and, therefore, who should pay how much at the end of a month. If there were two or more calls for reservations for the same time, the co-owner having the least number of hours on the docket was to have priority in the use of the ship.

By the time we got halfway down the wall, under the cellar steps, we had placed the expenses of operating the plane in two categories: First: Capital Expenses which were to be shared equally since they did not depend upon the number of hours flown. These were the so-called "fixed costs"—hangar rent, insurance for damage on the ground, major improvements, new instruments and repairs to instruments. Second: Variable Costs which were to be paid on a pro rata basis, depending on the number of hours each of the owners used the plane: gasoline, oil, repairs, flight insurance costs of hundred-hour checks and major overhauls were included in this heading.

In practice, we found on three occasions where a conflict developed that two fellows could use the plane for the same business trip, as when Hugh had to go to Hartford and Bill to Boston; Hugh just dropped off at Brainard Field in Hartford and Bill picked him up on the way home that afternoon, and several times they all went tootling off together on hunting trips.

Figuring out the costs of the Cessna after a year's operation, the boys found that they were operating a bigger airplane in the syndicate more cheaply than they could each operate their separate small planes, yet the larger plane far outperformed the little ones.

Into each life some rain must fall; one of the co-owners,

Bob, broke the bad news: he had to drop out of the syndicate since he was being transferred to the Midwest. The others then had two possible alternatives: either the remaining partners could buy out the interest of the withdrawing partner, or a new partner might be brought into the syndicate. The three remaining partners recognized the hazard of the latter choice: that, in a relationship like theirs things are pretty finely balanced personality-wise, and they had to be careful not to bring in a new "partner" who might disrupt the balance and get everyone fighting. They settled it directly. They paid off Bob's investment and carried on themselves, since they were at that time in the chips, and, for that matter, still are.

This is a problem that must be solved individually, however, and no one answer could fit all the problems that might arise, but it can be done.

Besides this small group I know of several large syndicates operating as "flying clubs" in which there are thirty or forty active members, who not only learned to fly, but continue to fly cheaply, purely for fun. A forty-man club shells out only fifty bucks a head for a two thousand dollar airplane! If you can't afford to pay a buck a week to fly, you can join the Civil Air Patrol Squadron in your neighborhood. Sometimes they will teach you gratis. There's always some angle you can figure out. Like the poker players say, the deal depends on the dealer.

13. Spring Fever

In a rash moment (while we were painting the bottom of his twenty-six-foot sea skiff), a boat-owning buddy confided to me that the trouble with owning a boat was that each year he wanted a bigger one. Along about the time the sap begins to rise in the trees, and birds and bees begin to act like birds and bees, the urge sets in to look around for a trade deal—a little more beam, maybe, or more speed. My boat owner now has a forty-six foot cruiser. I used to laugh at him until I learned the hard way that the same kind of pressure builds up in a pilot's boiler, too. When the weather turned warm and the light planes blossomed out like May flies, I began to look around for a plane that had more passenger space, some nifty radio equipment, or a faster cruise or—well, something new! Boats and planes have lots of things in common. Fickle owners and their truculent wives.

Before I could take the plunge anew, I had to solve a problem: after my whimsical purchase of the 140, my wife hated flying and airplanes in general and the little 140 in particular; it seems that she figured I was flying around in her mink stole, and she wasn't fixin' to put up with any investments in a new tin bird until she had that stole. So, like the coward I am, I secretly subscribed to aircraft trading papers at the office and on week-ends began to drift into new airports, looking for four-place planes—you know—just browsing.

Watching the advertisements for used planes, I began to cover the Eastern United States looking for the plane that might fill my requirements—cost three to four thousand dollars, carry four fellows, their rods, guns and maybe on occasion, my wife and family.

When my oldest boy's grades were good, I took him along but, when they weren't up to par, I left him home to hit the books and took some of my friends along for the ride. Several of the fellows who went with me as a lark became converts to flying, both for business and recreation, even though they had razzed me mercilessly when I first started to learn. Two of them now have their own planes; all they needed was the right introduction to flying.

At a dinner party one Friday night, for instance, a traveling salesman friend of mine was telling me how tired he was. "My territory covers from Albany to Wilmington. I just got in from Binghamton this afternoon and have to go to Albany tomorrow. Man, I'm beat!"

"My friend," I answered, munching a stalk of celery, "you need an airplane."

"Hunh, with all these turnpikes and freeways, an airplane would be ridiculous for me," he said. "I can average sixty miles an hour, so what good would an airplane be?"

"Come with me tomorrow," I invited. "I want to look at a plane in Albany, and you would be a welcome guest."

He was reluctant, but nevertheless agreed—provided I didn't tell his wife—and the next morning at nine-thirty we strapped on the 140, fired her up, and took off. As we

climbed out of Wings, I filed a flight plan by radio with
North Philadelphia: to Poughkeepsie direct, then up the
Hudson River to Albany. One hour and forty-seven minutes after we took off from Wings we were cleared for a
landing by Albany Tower. We rented a car and, while I
closed our flight plan and looked over the plane that was
for sale, he transacted his business. By two o'clock we were
back at Wings, having a hamburger and a cup of coffee at
the snack bar.

"How much does it cost to run one of those things?" he
asked, nodding at the planes tied down on the line. I bor-
rowed a pencil from the waitress and figured it out on the
back of a doily. "Four hours' flying time at five gallons an
hour is twenty gallons of gas, which cost thirty-eight cents
a gallon or seven dollars and sixty cents, plus a quart of
oil for two bits, makes it seven dollars and eighty-five
cents."

"That's a lot cheaper than my Buick, and not a toll
charge, either," he said seriously, reaching for the doily.

"That's right," I answered, lighting a cigarette, "and
you never had such a view of the Hudson Valley before,
either."

"I'm not thinking of the view as much as the fact that
I could sure cover a lot more territory in a plane, make
more money, and spend more time in the home office."

I didn't argue with him. After all, he's a businessman
and I'm a romantic vagabond by inclination.

About this time I got a jolt from my favorite mechanic,
plane-sitter and aeronautical wet nurse.

I had kind of a date to fly to New Mexico in the *Eagle*,
and, since I had put in a lot of winter flying, I decided to
have the plane checked over before I struck out for the

Raton Pass, a policy I always follow when I am going to cover a long distance; so, into the shop she went.

The engine was in excellent shape, the controls were perfect, the radio O. K. Then we tested the fabric on the wings.

Fabric is tested by a plunger-type gauge that punches a little round hole and registers the amount of pressure or force required to penetrate. When the fabric is new and strong, the gauge reads "in the green"; the easier it is to push through the line, the more towards the "red" side the gauge will read.

When we put the gauge on the ancient wings of the *Legal Eagle*, it went on through like a pencil through wet Kleenex. It didn't register at all.

Norb looked over his shoulder at me from his perch atop the ladder as I stood open-mouthed on the ground below him.

"Seems like this pigeon is fixin' to molt," he observed wryly, punching a series of holes in the top surface of the wings like this: "pop . . . pop . . . pop . . . pop."

"Yeah," I thought, "seems like this pigeon is going to go south with the money I was going to use to go west."

Reluctantly I put the nine-year-old plane in the shop for a month to get its first new set of wings, and ordered the shop to make a complete overhaul from prop to tailwheel, figuring that we might as well go whole hog while she was in dry dock.

Being without a plane for the first time since I got my license was a most distressing experience. I didn't know what to do with myself on the week-ends. I started snapping at the kids again and was generally miserable.

Once in a while when the feeling got too bad, I would go over to Wings and just hang around watching airplanes—and every so often I would lay down a couple of plasters and buy myself some time just to get up there in heaven for a little while, anyhow. I found that I wasn't just looking at planes. I was now really looking for the plane for me; I had a case of new-plane-itis, and I had it bad. Everyone knew it before I did. My wife just looked at me and sighed, and the airplane sellers called me at home and in the office. I wrote to all the airplane trading papers and subscribed to "Fliers' Market," a listing of used airplanes for sale. I corresponded with Powers and George, the aircraft brokers in New York.

On my quest for a new family jalopy of the air, I flew everything from single-place Mooney Mites to four-place Bonanzas whose owners were, in turn, looking for something new; for they too were undergoing the spring affliction, trading fever, the same way I was. As I flew each new plane I kept a record of it in my log for future reference, so that I could make comparisons of what they were like, how easy they were to fly, and especially how much they cost to buy and to operate. I made some interesting discoveries for myself about some of the planes that have had reputations around the hangar-flying meetings. And I finally found the perfect plane for the week-end pilot, about which I shall tell you.

Looking through my logbook, I see notes on all the planes I have flown, which are representative of what you can buy, both used and new, and most of the entries recall the memories of those flights as if it were yesterday.

Bob Angeli used to kid me, saying that I would fly anything beginning with "A"—a Cessna, a Piper, a Swift— so let's start with a real "A," the Aeronca.

The Aeronautical Corporation of America has come

and gone since 1930, leaving in its wake a passel of airplanes that were colorful, inexpensive, reliable and easy to fly. An awful lot of the older fliers mourn the passing of the company, one of the first catering to private flying, and remember warmly the planes that came aborning called Aeroncas.

I have never seen a C-2 Aeronca in the flesh, because they were produced about 1930, and I don't think any are left, unless they have been properly embalmed and placed under glass in some museum for future generations to see, like the "Tom Thumb" locomotive. The C-2's were little more than powered kites, being single seaters with twenty-eight- (yes, I said twenty-eight) horsepower engines.

Then, about 1931, Aeronca produced its C-3 model, said to be a "great improvement" over the previous year's; its power was upped to forty horsepower, a windshield was added, and its capacity was increased from one to two idiots.

I ran across one of these creations at a small airport in Virginia, and strolled over to examine it and see if it was for real. I'm still not sure.

It is hard to describe the C-3 to a completely sober person because it sounds so confounded improbable. Think of a pregnant guppy with wings, that's a start. Atop the stubby wing was a triangular mounting, the apex of which secured bracing wires extending outwards in each direction halfway down the wings, obviously to keep them from falling off when the airplane was on the ground. From the bottom of the fuselage another maze of wires of the type and character of those found at the extreme right side of a concert grand piano stretched upwards and outwards to meet the ones on top somewhere inside the wing. The tail assembly was held in position by another set of wires.

The C-3 had so many external bracing wires holding it together that I figured in a dive it would sound as if some angel on high had dropped his harp, which would probably play "Nearer My God to Thee" all the way down to the "Amen."

To get into the cockpit you had to bend double and wiggle a little, and once you were inside, the ground was only six inches below your own tail assembly. The propeller was about three feet long and struck me as being perfectly ridiculous—but then so did the whole plane. No brakes, no tailwheel, no radio.

As I scrunched on my knees trying to peer into the working parts, I was accosted by the owner, a seemingly sane individual who asked me if I wanted to "take it around once," as they say. I demurred passionately but, after thinking it over for two or three seconds, agreed to ride as a passenger, so we got into it. The pilot induced some idler to pull over the toothpick-sized prop and soon we were headed for the grass runway, me feeling all the world as if I were trundling cross-country in a winged bathtub.

With much blasting of the propeller (this "blast" being about the same as you get from a large electric fan), rudder wagging and bobbing up and down like a kid on a sled, he finally got the little plane headed into the wind, and, to the mass funereal headshaking of all onlookers, we staggered into the air, the wide-open engine making about half the noise of my power lawn mower at home. We went around the pattern only once, but that was enough.

All during the flight he kept leaning over to me and shouting "What did you say?" I wasn't talking to him; I was repeating the Twenty-third Psalm over and over. It did the trick; we got back in one piece; I fell out of the plane and rolled to safety; the last I saw he was flying off towards the North with a gaggle of geese following him, probably thinking it was Mother.

Aeronca made its post-war reputation with three light planes—the Chief, the Sedan and the Champion, of which there are many still cutting aerial didos all over the country.

The Chief was originally designed by one Dutch Darrin, who designed the Kaiser and Frazer automobiles, as well as many custom automobile bodies for movie stars on the West Coast. Side by side two seaters, they were underpowered by today's standards, but were trend-setters in the light-plane trade. With fifty horsepower they had slow cruising speeds, and even later with sixty-horsepower engines, they didn't sell enough to keep the line going, although there are still a lot of them around. I flew two of them, but decided they weren't for me, after I had been spoiled by the 140. You can get them for $750 and up.

The Sedan was produced to invade the four-place plane market, and was the first really low-priced plane made for private owners. It looked like a grown-up cross between the C-3 and the Chief—lumpy, yet roomy and comfortable. Doc Haines, who is literally the Big Mahoff of the Ocean City, N. J., Airport Association (he weighs about two hundred and thirty pounds), flies his Sedan all over and takes it to Florida each winter. A man his size hasn't been able to get a plane that will fit him for a reasonable price since Aeronca folded. As he said to me one time, "All you can buy nowadays for that dough is boys' sizes." This is a good airplane, selling used for $2250 to $3500.

The Aeronca Champion originally came out as a tandem trainer with sixty-five horsepower soon after World War II and a lot of them were gobbled up by flight schools and private individuals. Later an eighty-five-horsepower Continental was the standard engine for the plane, giving it about a hundred-and-five mph cruise, with slow landing speed but tremendous short field performance—a real "forgiving" airplane.

A friend of mine who runs a filling station purchased an old Aeronca Champion for about eight hundred bucks and learned to fly in it, just as I did in the 140. After getting his license, he flew to the Poconos for a week-end, and somewhere along the line en route home, he ran into a weather front which put him down at a small airport for what he expected would be a couple of hours. After tying the plane down securely, he went into the operations office for a smoke and cup of coffee, which he was enjoying, along with some hangar flying with the boys, when they noticed a loud rattling on the roof overhead.

"Hail?" asked one of the gab-festers, as five pairs of feet hit the floor at once, and the pilots ran to the window. Hail it was, as big as bullets, and having the same effect on the ancient fabric of the plane tied down outside the office. When the storm passed, the "Champ" looked like a toy that had been hit by a charge of buckshot. The wings were in tatters; so was the fuselage. The plane was a wreck.

It took a week to truck the bare-spar plane back to its home field, where it was pushed into the far corner of a hangar far from prying eyes to see. Jack couldn't afford the expense of having the plane recovered, but, "Where there is a will," as they say; he resolved to recover the plane himself. He towed it to his gasoline station and, so help me, recovered it, doped it, painted it and got it back into the air in five weeks! The CAA inspector said the job was perfect, and today the plane is flying regularly.

I recommend this model highly, except that I don't like the tandem seating arrangement, which is purely a personal complaint. This plane is really a lady all the time.

Aeronca failed in business, as I have said, but the Champion was too good to die. A new company has taken over the grand old plane, now with a ninety-five-horse-power motor up front, and sells it for farm dusting and spraying. It cruises at a hundred and twelve mph and is a great tool for farmers, sort of a do-it-yourself bug killer kit.

Aeronca is dead—long live the Champion!

Talk to the average person about light-plane flying, and I'll give you eight to five that the words "Piper Cub" come up in the conversation within five minutes, and for a darn good reason—more people have learned to fly in Piper Cubs than any other airplane.

Besides basic training of pilots who were to wind up in P-38's over Rabaul and B-17's over Berlin, it also edged into the shooting war as an artillery spotter, liaison plane and winged jeep. Flying fifteen hundred feet over enemy lines, spotting targets, unarmed and unarmored, does not cause life insurance agents to mash their knuckles to a pulp on one's doorjamb, but a lot of fellows did it and came back unscathed, even though I couldn't bear to watch. In New Guinea, I saw J-2's deliver guns, gin and generals, landing on roads, beaches and clearings in the jungle.

The J-2 and the later J-3 have grown into quite an air

plane nowadays—from sixty-five to one hundred fifty horsepower—and the new "Super-Cub" can operate under almost any conditions. I wouldn't be surprised if they come out with one that will land upside down on the hangar ceiling like a fly.

The J-3 Cub is still used as a basic trainer at thousands of flying schools, and for a good reason—about the only way you can really get killed in one is to write a farewell note, hold the stick all the way forward with your knees, and close your eyes.

The J-3 is slow—it cruises at seventy mph—and is, therefore, ideal for student cross-country flights; for who, besides me, can get lost in a J-3, especially bucking a headwind? Tom flew a seventy-mile cross-country one day and took two hours and ten minutes to cover the distance because of thirty-eight-mph headwinds; his ground speed figured out to thirty-two mph, faster than a motor scooter, maybe, but not much.

Landing seems to be a slow motion affair: The J-3 stalls out at about thirty-five mph, and in a stiff wind you come in at a slow walk.

J-3's can be had for about $500, and, at that price, compares favorably with the smallest outboard motorboat or build-it-yourself plane kit.

I have flown ninety, a hundred and thirty-five, and a hundred and fifty-horsepower Super-Cubs, the big brothers of the old J-3, and all I can say is "wow." These Super-Cubs are sure out of the toy class for fair; the ninety-horsepower job cruises at a hundred mph, and the new 150 cruises at a hundred and ten. The latter will take off in a hundred feet with two adults aboard and climb about forty degrees, and I got an awful bump on the head when a Piper demonstrator landed a Super-Cub (equipped with the Whittaker dual gear) with the brakes on; I don't think we rolled ten feet.

In Maine I flew a Cub on floats, and I know a prospector who habitually flies a mere fifty feet away from the sheer walls of canyons dragging a scintillometer, searching for uranium. He often lands on the sides of hills or on the desert and flies in all kinds of weather. In Ohio I once watched a farmer dust his own fields like a professional, although he had never been in a plane until six months before. He told me that his Super-Cub was as valuable to him as a combine.

I have already recounted the time we got lost over Jersey in a Super-Cub because of a bum compass, or maybe I should say a poorly adjusted compass and bum flying, because that certainly wasn't the fault of the airplane. We often rent Super-Cubs in our business for aerial photography of auto accident locations and real estate developments, since the entire right side opens up, giving a wide area free from interference with the camera. Just hold on tight and don't let the camera blow out the window.

Somewhere in the accident reports discussed elsewhere in the book is one of a Cub that was nosed-up and the full story, as told to me, bears repeating.

The back seat of the Super-Cub can be removed to give a space of about eighteen cubic feet for cargo, very useful to farmers and ranchers, for using the plane like a pick-up truck. A farmer's wife, having decided to jaunt fifty miles to the general store to pick up some calico, a couple of salt blocks and a large can of paint, slipped into the family Cub, and prepared to aviate. About this time, Junior, seven and a half years old, set up a clamor that he wanted to go, despite the fact that there was no back seat, and, instead of belting him one and leaving him flat on his back, soft-hearted, soft-headed Mama let him get into the stripped-down cargo space, and off they went, with a whoop and a holler.

On the way home, since the back of the Cub was jammed full of hard and soft goods, Junior had to sit in Ma's lap, like a warm Elmer Snerd, which gave him a better view than he had ever had, but, in trying to shoot a landing back at their South Forty, Mother suddenly found to her surprise that because of Junior's knees, the stick wouldn't come back enough to flare out and Mom, Junior, the salt, calico and paint, after three bounces, wound up in a lump against the firewall. Said calico, paint, salt, Ma's dentures and the prop were ruined. Junior came out of it without a bruise. Until Pop came home.

Somewhere between the J-3 and the Super-Cub, Piper made a three place Piper Cruiser, later a Super-Cruiser; then the four-place Pacer came off the ramp. These are all terrific planes, and many of them are still around for $2000 or less, depending on their condition, of course.

The original PA 20 Pacer was the 125, powered with a Lycoming a hundred-and-twenty-five-horsepower engine. Later it came out in an improved model known as the 135—a stubby, four-place high-performance plane that cruised about a hundred and twenty-five mph. It was a success but, when someone at Lock Haven moved the main gear aft and put a nose wheel on to produce a tricycle gear that took the nasty part out of cross-wind operation, the Piper people suddenly found that they had a real bomb. For a few years the PA 20 Pacer and its variation, named the **PA 22** Tri-Pacer, were made side by side, but the tricycle gear model sold so much better that, as of 1956, the Tri-Pacer alone is produced in this class.

I have flown Tri-Pacers to New York and Washington and take my hat off to their designers, for the Tri-Pacer is all that its ads say it is, with simplified controls, comfortable pilot and passenger accommodations, speed, quietness and dependability. My father-in-law, who flew in the first World War and since that time has hated airplanes, had never been in a modern one until he was reconverted by flying a Tri-Pacer ground to ground with Frank Mayock at his side merely telling him what to do. His first comment: "I missed the wind in my face."

This is one hell of an airplane any way you look at it and can be had, used, for $3500.

Not long ago a friend of mine bought a new hundred-and-fifty-horsepower Tri-Pacer, upon which he painted the name "Fifi," to the amusement of the airport loafers. I think that his choice of a French girl's name was good, though, for he told me the reason: "She looks perky and chic, is a wonderful playmate and, when I touch her right, she jumps." Who's to argue?

The low-wing all-metal Globe Swift is the hot rod of private flying, a little firecracker carrying two people at a fast and furious pace through the sky. This plane appeals to me like nobody's business—sleek, with retractable gear and having excellent visibility, looking, feeling and flying all the world like a small fighter plane. Since I had my heart set on a four-place plane and the only Swift that I could buy in my neck of the woods had an eighty-five-horsepower engine (with which it seems un-

der-powered), I didn't strain to hock my banjo to raise
the money. But if it had been the hundred-and-twenty-
five or hundred-and-forty-five horsepower model, I am
afraid that I would have been a gone goose. The Swift's
only drawback for a week-end pilot is that it lands faster
than almost any other plane, stalling out at about sixty
mph, which means that the approach and landing must
be always perfectly executed in a small field, otherwise
you roll out through trees, rocks or whatever else is at the
far end of the strip, but an experienced Swift pilot seldom complains about this factor because he knows how to
handle the ship. Swifts are available, used, for $1500 to
$3000, and are the answer for traveling salesmen and
other fellows who want to get there in a hurry. It
wouldn't take me much to be a Swift nut.

Another nifty plane that is back in production after a
five-year lapse is the widely used Bellanca—a high-performance, low-wing, four-place plane with retractable
gear and flaps. I almost bought the one I flew, but pulled
back because I didn't like the wooden fuselage; as a
Cessna bug, I am partial to metal ones. For $4000 you
can get a pretty good Bellanca, but the model I flew was
too old and worn out to suit me; I was afraid that, if the
termites ever stopped holding hands, the plane would
fall apart. Recently I flew one in good shape to Easton,
Maryland, and learned to respect its flyability and got a
new slant on the plane. Boy, oh, boy, can the good one
fly! The owner wouldn't even talk to me about selling it,
even for $4000, so I forgot it.

The Culver Cadet is a two-place, low-wing plane, one
of the first with retractable gear. It cruises at about a

hundred and fifty mph, and lands at about sixty-five mph, so it is considered a pretty "hot" airplane for week-end pilots. I rode one on the right side, but wasn't really interested, because it was too small for my needs.

Cadets are no longer made at this writing, but used ones are still around for reasonable prices, about the same as 140's. I wouldn't recommend this plane for the average person, but it surely is the first of the high performance light planes that have recently been brought to such a high degree of efficiency since 1945.

The first Cadet I saw was painted bright red and the cockpit was jammed with electronic instruments. It was 1945, in the Philippine Islands, as I recall, on the hangar deck of an aircraft carrier. My host, who had invited me aboard to take a shower and eat some real food that we poor relations in PT's never got on the beach, noticed my interest in the little plane nestled down among the huge F6F's and TBF's that were jammed into the floating hangar in sort of a systematic chaos.

"O. K.," I said to him, "I give up. What is it?"

He ran his hand along the smooth fuselage of the little low-winged plane, much as one might pat a family puppy.

"That is a drone aircraft," he answered. "We had several of them to train gunners for anti-aircraft work. Someday a so-and-so will hit it with a thirty-seven-millimeter or a fifty-caliber machine gun."

"Expendable, eh," I mused to him.

"To the Navy, yes, but not to me," he said. "I used to fly one of these back home. Now some guy will sit on the deck and fly it by radio control like a kite or a power model. War sure is Hell."

A friend of mine just picked one up for $1500 with VHF radio in it, and, the last I heard, was flying to Las Vegas or New Orleans, I forget which. Anyhow, someplace with gorgeous girls. He's a bachelor.

About 1945 a new type of airplane came on the American scene—the so-called "single control" light plane. Ercoupe directed its sales energies towards non-fliers on this slant: "The Ercoupe has no rudder pedals, only a wheel. You drive it like a car, both on the ground and in the air." The idea that it could not be spun and need not be stalled in to land, since it had a tricycle landing gear, went over big and seems to have been the forerunner of light-plane tricycle gear, which is rapidly becoming universal. It made an impression on those people who wanted to fly their own planes, but despite the sales pitch, sales got slow and Ercoupe is no longer a current production. Nevertheless, there are many of the airplanes around for $1500, and for a reasonable investment a big new engine can be installed and the plane's performance improved.

The Ercoupe has fixed tricycle gear, metal body, fabric-covered wings, is low-wing with a two-place cockpit. It is a good airplane for cloud loafers, although I like standard controls better. Incidentally, there is a "rudder kit" available for this plane, so you can have conventional controls installed, a great improvement, I think.

The one I flew averaged about a hundred and five mph, which is on the slow side for a plane, but a heck of a lot faster than a car—even a Mercedes-Benz—and again, this is a plane that *anyone* can fly. If one is around for a reasonable price, don't be hesitant about latching on to it.

Unless he knows airplanes pretty well, the average person can't tell the difference between a Luscombe and a

Cessna 140 when he sees them on the ground or in the air.

The Luscombe is also a high wing, all metal monoplane, and its general performance is about the same as the Cessna. However, the Luscombe has a stick control, while the 140 has a wheel, and there is not as much space in the cabin for storing maps and small packages.

It is a good little airplane, found all over the country, used for pipe-line flying, charter work and pleasure trips. A reliable, trustworthy work horse, unfortunately no longer made. You can get them for prices ranging from $1100 to $1500. This is a nice little plane, but one gave me a scare from which I have never fully recovered.

The owner and I were flying some lazy eights about three thousand feet over Ambler when I remarked how much control he seemed to have near the stall.

"Oh, yes," he said, "this plane has lots of lateral control at all speeds," at which he waggled the stick by way of illustration. Suddenly behind us there was a loud bang, sounding for all the world as if someone had dropped a Belgian block inside the fuselage. For five minutes that seemed an eternity, we gingerly flew back to Wings and landed, engaging meanwhile in absolutely no conversation whatsoever until she stopped rolling. Then we both began to breathe again and asked each other, "What was *that*?"

We examined that plane inside and out and never did find out what made the noise; so we concluded that we had hit a bird, although that's only a guess. Could have been Bridey Murphy.

One of my new-found friends makes his living flying Super-DC-8s to Europe and the Middle East, about as glamorous a way to make a buck as most of us can imagine, yet he looks upon his vocation as humdrum and considers it to be about as thrilling as driving a bus. The moment he comes home he climbs into his own plane and cleans out the cobwebs which he claims develop after two weeks of staring at the maze of instruments in the "office" of the DC-8. He is six feet two inches tall and weighs two hundred pounds. His personal plane is a Mooney Mite.

The "Mite" is well-named, being a shade over seventeen feet long, one-place, low-wing, with retractable tricycle gear and an open cockpit covered by a sliding hatch à la World War II fighter planes. It has the most rakish appearance anyone ever built into a plane. It personifies aerial derring-do, and the only thing that detracts from its sleek fighter-plane appearance is that you keep looking to see where to wind up the mainspring.

The Mite is no tinker-toy, though. It is a real airplane, and exciting to fly; the only trouble is that there isn't enough room in it for two people, even if they are midgets. My check-out in the Mite made me sympathize with the boys who went from dual trainers to single-engine fighters during the war: the only instruction I got was Al saying, "This is the gear handle; this is the flap handle; pick up the gear the moment you break ground, trim out at a hundred and twenty-five, approach at seventy-five, drop gear and flaps, come over the fence at sixty, and land."

Cramming my two hundred pounds of fighting fury into the tiny cockpit was something like putting on a girdle, but I finally got myself down on the seat and fastened the strap, wondering momentarily how I was going to get out later. Have to turn the plane upside down and shake me out, probably.

Al stood at the prop, the hub of which was at the height of his belt buckle, and yelled, "Switch off?"

"Off," I replied, checking the ignition. He pulled the prop over twice and the sixty-five-horsepower Lycoming engine went "whooshiticka—whooshiticka."

"Contact?" he said, poised to snap the prop.

"She's hot," I answered, throwing the switch and looking up at him.

"Brroom!" she went, like a motorcycle, and, as Al waved me on, I taxied to the runway. After the usual check-off procedure, I reached up with both hands behind my ears and slid the transparent hatch into place, "swish—click." Visibility was terrific, and the air was clear of planes. I opened the throttle, headed down the strip into the wind, and fed her the coal. Being so close to the ground, I felt as if I were going two hundred miles an hour, but the airspeed indicator read 50 when I eased back on the stick and reached for the gear-retracting lever. She broke ground and I threw the lever with a fast motion—whoop!—the gear was up like that, and it was "Nellie, bar the gate!" You have to see the Mooney gear come up to believe it—even then you have your doubts, for it retracts as fast as the guy behind me blows his horn when the light turns green.

I was at two thousand feet before I even began to relax: first my toes came uncurled, shoes and all, and last, my hair stopped sticking up like cactus spines.

I tried a few turns, did some stalls and tried to side-slip, just to get the feel of the little ship. I say, "tried to sideslip," because the rudder pedals wouldn't travel far enough to make the plane slip. Oh, yes, when I cut the throttle back to stall, a little red disc began to wigwag madly before my eyes and gave me quite a start. I thought for a moment that the panel was going to spill quarters into my lap.

The approach was nifty, red flag waving and all, and, when I got the gear down, the flag dropped as though a taxi meter went off. On final I got the flaps down, came over the fence at fifty-five mph, and eased onto the runway, feeling altogether like Joe Foss.

When I slid the hatch back and hunched out of the cockpit, there was a sucking noise, then a "pop," like opening a bottle of champagne. I can see why Al likes to fly the Mite after horsing a big jet over the Ocean.

These planes can be had for $2000 or so, used, and are the beans for hermits or people who want to be alone.

Last week I saw a used four-place Mark 20, which is a small Bonanza-type four-place airplane, costing twelve grand, not yet available used. That's a nice plane, but the Mite has a special appeal all its own.

The low-wing all-metal Navion has been a favorite personal and business plane since it first came out after World War II, built by North American Aviation. Later the manufacture was taken over by Ryan, the power was beefed up and performance was improved. I don't know why it is no longer built, but suspect that the Bonanza sand-bagged it consumerwise, as they say in the advertising dodge.

The Navion is a nice, stable plane, easy to fly, having the appearance of an automobile with wings, except that it has no door. Instead, the roof slides back like the hatch on the Mooney Mite. If you land in the rain, you are going to get your dome damp, and the seats will get wet, which is a bad feature, and my wife objects to the unladylike aspects of getting aboard by the two high steps ahead of the wing; it is no place for a short tight skirt. I have never heard men complain, though, come to think of it.

Despite these purely personal criticisms, the Navion is a roomy and comfortable machine, and a steal at $5000, for which it is available, used, in the two-hundred-and-five-horsepower model.

A friend of mine who crosses the U.S.A. every six months in his Navion, with his wife and three kids, swears that it is the greatest plane ever made, and my partner wants one so much he can taste it.

The first time I took off with Angeli in a Navion and had about four hundred feet altitude, I heard a loud bump-bump under the plane. I blanched as the thought crossed my mind that someone was caught underneath and was knocking for help, but Bob laughed and explained that the sound was made by the wheels coming up into the wells.

It's things like that that make me nervous.

"B is for Business," as they say in my small son's school-books, and "B is for Bonanza," for Bonanza is the business plane for single-engine operation all over the country. What Cadillac has stood for, since World War II, in the automobile industry, the Beechcraft Bonanza has represented as a personal plane; it has "class." It has been for ten years the greatest single-engine plane around in terms of performance, although other manufacturers are trying to design planes to the same specifications at the present writing. If I were rich, or if I had a business where I needed fast transportation, it would be a Bonanza.

This speedy single-engine, low-wing, four-place plane with the unique butterfly tail, has an undeserved bad reputation for being a hard plane to fly, a killer, a trap for the unwary; and, in justification of their position, the self-appointed prophets of Bonanza-doom cite fatality reports where people were killed in Bonanzas. As a result my partner adamantly refuses to step into one, and many others make faces and shake their heads nervously if the name "Bonanza" comes up in casual conversation.

"The wings come off," they say.

"It oscillates."

Hogwash! All of it.

In my opinion this attitude harks back to the chronic fear of flying that has been developed in our marrow by promoters of hysteria, coupled with the widespread desire of most new fliers to have a "forgiving" airplane. These people want an airplane that will fly low and slow, and they get into an emotional swivel as soon as they hear that a plane will cruise over a hundred and seventy-five mph. The whole idea that a Bonanza is tricky to fly is the end result of these distorted ideas.

I am a great admirer of Bonanzas, having flown them to Boston, Chicago and Norfolk, Virginia, on numerous occasions. Except for the fact that there are more gadgets to monkey around with—cowl flaps, adjustable propeller, mixture controls, retractable gears and automatic flaps— the Bonanza is one of the easiest, most comfortable and relaxing planes to fly that I have ever been in. It cruises at a hundred and seventy-five (the new model G claims a hundred and ninety-five), yet lands at fifty-five mph. It can take off and land on any field that is reasonably smooth, and, in a pinch, can be landed, wheels up, on rough surfaces in a short space, without too much damage to the plane and none to the occupants.

The chief pilot at Wings put a Bonanza through its paces for me when I was checking out, and opened my eyes to its possibilities. On take-off, he opened the throttle, hauled back on the wheel at fifty-five mph, and we broke ground. The same instant he hit the gear switch and the wheels slammed into their wells; he set the prop pitch, holding the nose up to maintain seventy-five mph air-speed and we went up to eight hundred feet like a shot out of a gun. When we came into the pattern, he dropped the gear and flaps, set the prop in low pitch, held her at seventy-five all the way down, placed her so that she set-tled onto the end of the runway and slammed on the brakes. Two hundred feet down the macadam we stopped.

I am a little conservative on both take-offs and land-ings, but the Beech will go in on an approach just about where you point it, and, one thing I know, won't float all the way across the field even on a hot summer day.

Where does the bad reputation come from? First of all, the "Banana" is an exceptionally clean airplane. There are no external bumps or knobs to distort the air flow and create skin friction; therefore, if the nose drops, airspeed builds up extremely rapidly, although the pilot can correct the attitude of the plane and slow down. If a noninstrument pilot gets into IFR conditions and the nose drops, it is clear that a high-speed spiral dive can develop quickly. In an effort to slow the plane, the tense pilot may haul the wheel back abruptly, a bad technique at exces-sively high speed, and anything can happen. Tough luck all around. But, for a proficient pilot, the nose-down atti-tude can't be too dangerous. Beech test pilots spin Bo-nanzas all the time and recover without hurting the plane.

So, a conclusion: if you stay out of that IFR weather, as

private pilots must do anyhow, the Bonanza is a safe machine, designed to perform like nobody's business.

And the snide malarkey about the butterfly tail making it "oscillate" is so much jazz, too! Any really clean, fast airplane will "hunt" as it whips through the air currents and density gradients of the atmosphere. The earlier Bonanzas did shake the bone a bit; the newer ones with some slight design changes don't do it quite so much, no more than a Navion, for instance. In any event, it is not dangerous, not uncomfortable and certainly not excessive.

There is no more delightful sensation than flying a Bonanza at two thousand feet over the flat farm land of the Eastern Seaboard, for in no other plane does one have the sensation of speed that compares to such a ride.

New, it costs $70,000, the price of a home in the suburbs, but they are available used, from $6,000 up.

As you may have guessed by now, I yield to no one in my admiration for the magnificent airplanes put out by Dwane Wallace and his cohorts in Wichita. I think that, for the low-cost personal plane to be flown by the casual or week-end pilot, the Cessna is the outstanding product of our day.

Cessna pioneered the cheaper all-metal light plane, which can stand outside in all kinds of weather, including hail, without being demolished by the elements. Its spring steel landing gear is not only strong but, as far as I know, unbreakable; it is equally trouble-free. Cessnas are roomier inside than any other comparable plane, and are cheaper to operate than a Ford car. They will cruise at a hundred and twenty, yet can be slowed down to forty-five, and fly as steady as a rock aloft with their high wing construction.

There are, of course, several models of the Cessna in widespread use at the present time. The old two-place models, the 120 and 140, were similar, except that the 120 did not have an electrical system (lights, starter, radio) and flaps, whereas the 140 did. Later models of the 140 have metal wings, and many 120's have had metal wings and electrical systems installed, which improve them a great deal.

The 140 series, like the one I have, had a big brother, the 170, which is a four-place plane with a hundred-and-forty horsepower up front; otherwise, it is very similar to the 140 in its flight characteristics. A few years back the 170 B came out, essentially the same all-metal plane, except that it has flaps that are enormous. The original 170's had little skinny flaps like those on the 140's, amounting to little more than "spoilers." But, with the newest ones, on an approach the pilot can steepen the glide angle and cut down the tendency to "float" which is inherent in the wants-to-fly Cessnas.

The so-called para-flaps on the 170 B create so much drag that you can dive like the old German Stukas right down at the field and still never go over seventy-five or eighty mph. The first time I flew a B, I tested out the flaps at three thousand feet, and when I hauled up the flap-handle it appeared that the entire wing was pulling off and it scared hell out of me. They really are big!

Even not using flaps, I find that, if it is a hot day, I can fly the plane right into the ground in a wheel landing without harm to the spring steel gear. Since the Cessnas fly so easily, it is not unusual on a hot day to flare out in a conventional full stall landing and then float all the way across the field four feet above the runway before she finally stalls out and lands. I kill the floating tendency by flying the plane right at the end of the runway at a speed well above the stall, then, just as the wheels touch, shove hard forward against the control wheel, raising the tail and forcing the plane against the ground. This maneuver is guaranteed to terrorize the most phlegmatic passenger unless you warn him that you are going to do it, but is really quite safe, since all you are doing is insuring: one, that the plane gets down; two, stays down; and three, slows down. As soon as the speed sloughs off, the tail will drop of its own accord.

The Cessna 180 is a still bigger brother, like the 170 inside, but with more power, an adjustable prop and a somewhat richer interior. It sells, used, for $10,000 or so. The two-hundred-twenty-five-horsepower engine moves the 180 along at a hundred and fifty mph, yet lands at forty-five. This plane is a few miles slower than the Bonanza but, new, costs only $13,000, a little more than half as much as the Beech, and there is no retractable gear to go out of whack. I advise all small businessmen and traveling salesmen to look into this baby—it's a cinch to fly.

The Cessna 195, now discontinued, was a high-performance five-passenger executive plane, designed to compete both in speed and luxury with the Bonanza, which didn't work out. It is the only Cessna that I think is ugly, and it was too expensive for the competitive Beechcraft. Perhaps people felt like the fellow that said, "If I had enough money to get married, I'd buy a car." In their case, if they had enough money to buy and operate a Cessna 195, they bought a Bonanza. Just a guess on my part.

In 1956, Cessna, apparently feeling the pinch because

Piper was knocking their brains out with the PA 22 (the Tri-Pacer) which came equipped with a tricycle landing gear and an advertising gimmick to match which appealed to new fliers, redesigned the 170 and 180 into two new tricycle-geared models, the 172 and 182 respectively, and later brought out the Cessna 150 which is essentially a Cessna 140 with a nose wheel, like its big brothers.

Despite what would at first seem to be an obvious drag created by the nose wheel hanging out in front like a bulbous proboscis, there doesn't seem to be any appreciable difference in the flying or handling qualities of the 150, 172 or 182 in the air, and there is no doubt in anyone's mind, after having essayed a gusty cross-wind landing, that the tricycle gear is the greatest invention since the wired brassière. Now the Cessnas have the same advertising gimmick as the Pipers—anyone can fly a tricycle-gear plane, and they advertise widely in all the national magazines, "Who, *me* fly?"

14. So I Wrote This Book

As they say in the comic strips, "Husbands are a sorry lot." No sooner does the one who is laughingly referred to as "the head of the family" get a few bucks ahead on the fiscal carousel than the *status* is returned to *quo* by his helpmeet who sallies forth on her white charger-plate and arranges to put the money into circulation again. Share the wealth. Spread the dough around. Keep those silver dollars rolling from man to man. Go for broke. And another notch is carved into the checkbook.

My problem came to a head when, through some grotesque error, my wife found that I had accumulated a little balance in the account and began to itch for a new car. "Look," she would say, after throwing a steak into me, lighting my cigar and slipping into something seductive, "here's a Lincoln for sale at the ridiculously low price of forty-nine ninety-eight. We can get eighteen-fifty for the old car and borrow a little and have delivery by Friday. Nice, huh? O. K., huh? C'mon, huh?"

I didn't tell her I had the money and that, as far as I was concerned, it was already earmarked for a Cessna 170

B, listed for sale at Wings for fifty-five hundred dollars, with all kinds of radio and blind flying instruments. I had realized that there were two tough hurdles for me to surmount before the 170 was mine—the money was the first one, and you-know-who was the second, not to mention you-know-who's mother.

But I had it figured out: If I sold the *Eagle* for eighteen hundred and cleaned out the bank account, I could borrow the rest of the price and be in business, provided I scrimped, gave up smoking and going to the movies— and especially if I didn't buy a new car.

Therefore, when I got the steaks and negligee treatment, I knew that I was going to have to act fast, because it was clear that the big, beautiful brunette was serious about that lemon yellow hard-top, and she knows my weak points: I like steak, cigars and other things. Women are so sneaky.

Secretly, inwardly keeping my own counsel, I made a decision: get the 170 before you give in to your frailties. I didn't tell my wife right away, though, because I can be pretty sneaky myself. Besides, I realized full well that a disclosure of my decision could be made only at the proper time, on the proper occasion, and in the proper manner, when lots of people were around to act as my protectors. In plain language, I wasn't going to spill the beans until I was pretty sure that my beloved wasn't going to blow a gasket.

This second phase of my problem, I calculated, could be solved by having a party. All I had to say was, "Let's have some people in on Saturday night," and the next thing I knew our lawn looked like the infield at Hialeah on Opening Day. Mention the word "party" to my wife, and she begins to spin like the turbine in a jet engine.

All around the lawn people were gathered into small groups, laughing and having fun, and it seemed that the psychological time was drawing near to drop the bomb about the 170. I pulled a few of the boys aside and gleefully filled them in on my plan, which they all agreed was the only way to handle the matter. By the time we broke up the confab, we had pretty well covered the proposition and its advantages for a family man and, suitably fortified and backed by their moral support, I set out to let Marianne know just where the bear stomped in the buckwheat.

When I saw her surrounded by guests and having a wonderful time, I had a sudden pang of conscience. "Not now," a little voice said. "Don't be a meanie and spoil her fun." And I didn't say a word.

The last of the guests finally departed, horns blaring and tires kicking gravel all over the driveway, and the two of us began to clean up the ash trays, the paper napkins, and the flotsam and jetsam that are left in the wake of a party.

"Didn't Helen have a good time?" Marianne asked, as she rinsed a stubby glass under the kitchen faucet.

"Yes, and Libby laughed the whole evening," I answered, opening the icebox door to pour a glass of buttermilk. "Glump," went the door, as I downed the drink, and I suddenly noticed that there was no conversation from my wife, although she was still in the room with me.

"You really *want* that 170, don't you?" she asked over the rim of a cup of coffee, staring at me intently.

"Yes, I guess I do," I answered, suddenly feeling pretty guilty about my childish plan—as if I didn't know she would have seen through it. "But there are other things that must come first." Whoops, that did it—I'll have to get her the car now.

"How long has it been since you have had to see a doctor?" she asked, putting her cup in the dishwasher.

I had to think for a minute. "Two years," I answered, remembering those men looking down at me with their grave expressions.

"That's right," she said, "two years. You haven't seen a doctor since you bought the airplane. You haven't taken an aspirin, or a sleeping pill, or an ulcer tablet or a tranquilizer capsule. You haven't had heartburn or dizzy spells." She took the empty glass from my limp hand and put it in the sink.

"You go ahead and buy that 170," she said. "It means more to me to have you well and happy than it does to have a new car or a mink coat or a yacht."

It was I who sat down to absorb the blow, not she—as I had planned it—and my head was spinning like a gyro. What a switch. What a woman! What a life!

"C'mon, Lindbergh," she said, taking my hand and leading me upstairs, "tomorrow will be a nice day for flying, but there's still some of tonight left."

Monday morning I wrote to Powers and George, the aircraft brokers in New York, and to "Fliers' Market" in Chicago, advertising the 140 for sale for seventeen hundred and fifty dollars. I had to move quickly to make the connection I had my eye on at Wings, and three weeks later pilots all over the country knew that the *Eagle* was for sale. I certainly got results; I was literally deluged with inquiries about the 140, but some of them offended me.

"Let's have the poop on your pot," said one.

"It's pretty old, how about cutting the price?" said another.

My Irish came up when I read those letters. Imagine calling that dainty little 140 a "pot," or saying she was "old." As far as I was concerned, people who didn't like airplanes any more than that would never get near my beloved Cessna.

Then I opened a letter postmarked in Bethlehem:

"I would like very much to buy your 140 but, since this will be the first plane I ever owned, I wonder if you would fly it to Bethlehem-Easton Airport, so my instructor can look it over?"

After the cold, calculating letters that had frosted my heart, this letter was a breath of spring. That letter-writer was in very much the same position I had been in when I bought Zero four four. Obviously he was a new pilot just starting out, and I knew she would be cared for like a lady.

I didn't write; I called him on the telephone. "Fly her up? Sure I will. Next Saturday."

The appointed day was clear and cool when my number-one boy and I climbed into the blue for the twenty-minute flight to the small airport near Bethlehem.

As we taxied up to the line, the prospective buyer—a young man—and his instructor were waiting for us. I saw excitement mirrored in the eyes of the student as he appraised the ship, and wondered if I had looked like that the first time I had seen it.

The instructor, who operated the field, reminded me somewhat of Bob Angeli, a clear-eyed young Air Force veteran whom I liked instantly, named Trigiani. For fifteen minutes he looked over the propeller and engine, and asked all sorts of questions. "The heck with the log-books," he said to me, "let's take her up and see how she flies. We'll go to Allentown-Bethlehem and try out the radio."

I eyed him speculatively. This was a practical guy. "I bet he is a darn good instructor," I thought to myself, as we climbed into the plane.

I felt strange. For the first time, I sat in the right-hand side as Trig flew the five-minute trip to Allentown, called in on the radio, and landed on Runway thirty-three. As we turned to go back to the take-off position, I noticed a new Cessna 172 standing on the Lehigh Aviation ramp.

"Whose is *that?*" I asked, pointing at the parked aircraft.

"That's our new Cessna 172; I'm a sub-dealer," he said, then added, with a grin, "Want to fly it?"

Asking me that was like asking a kid if he wanted a box-seat pass to the ball game, so Trig ran her over to the parking area, pulled on the brakes, and we jumped out.

While he was in the office getting the ignition keys, I examined the 172 closely.

"Gosh, this plane looks low to me. Won't the propeller strike the ground?" I asked, as Trig came out, keys in hand.

"Nope," said Trig, "she has plenty of clearance."

"How about a hard landing in a gusty wind on rough ground?" I asked, still an unbeliever.

"My friend, that's the same nose gear they put on the 310 model and it's not made of pewter. Sure you can bend it if you fly into a stone wall, but not on any landing field."

After we preflight-inspected the 172, I climbed in the great big left door and Trig in the right, not much differently than when entering an automobile. On the seat was a pile of advertisements that Cessna had begun to use in its sales approach, entitled "Who, *me* fly?" I threw them in the back seat—all but one which I swiped. What the heck, I was a prospect! For a few minutes we went over the cabin's layout, which I saw was generally trim, compact, with everything handy. Close to the ground nose down, the visibility ahead was phenomenal: I could see the concrete ramp about ten feet ahead of the prop.

When Trig gave me the sign, I yelled, "Clear," and hit the starter and the engine went "Brooooooom" in a bass voice. The tower gave taxi clearance over the VHF loudspeaker hidden in the roof of the cabin, so I carefully eased along the taxi strip, feeling as if I were driving in my beetle-like Volkswagen; there was nothing out front but the ground.

I ran the engine up, checked the mags, and went through the pre-take-off routine, then the tower cleared us for take-off. Once airborne, she performed beautifully. The airspeed indicator hung on 125 when we got her trimmed out, and in turns, stalls and slow-flight she was firm, stable and solid.

Finally we worked back into the pattern and were cleared to land, so I made one of my characteristically conservative approaches and hit the paving about one-third of the way down the runway, flaring out in a typical Cessna landing, but then I got a scare, for, despite my holding the wheel way back, the nose dropped down, down, down—Bump! and the steerable nose wheel glued onto the macadam.

"How do you like that gear?" he asked, as I gently braked to a stop with the individual toe brakes on the rudder pedals. "Makes landing pretty simple, doesn't it?"

"Yes, but I am still leery that these high-wing tricycle planes will tip over if you turn too fast or if there is a real bad cross wind when you come in.

"Tip over?" he answered scornfully, shaking his head. "Not this baby!"

"Yeah, you're a Cessna salesman, and I never heard a fish vendor yelling 'rotten fish,' yet," I answered doubtfully.

"Here," he said, "let me show you what this thing will do," and he took over the dual controls while I sat back and observed. We were rolling about 25 mph when he pushed hard right rudder and started the plane turning right on the taxi strip, then he stepped hard on the right brake pedal and pivoted the plane in its own length all the way around in a three hundred sixty-degree turn— swish—like that.

"How 'zat for ground handling?" he asked, like a kid with a new toy. "Still worried about tipping over?" My respect for the Cessna tricycle gear was mounting rapidly as he taxied to the end of the runway and asked the tower for permission to take off, which was promptly granted.

Trig reached down and pulled the big flap handle between us up two notches and opened the throttle, tugging at the wheel as we gathered speed down the black runway. I had my eye on the airspeed indicator on the panel in front of me, and when the needle got to forty-eight mph I looked out to see when we were going to take off—just in time to see the taxiway flash past forty feet below. Despite the fact that the throttle was wide open, the cabin was as quiet as Easter week in Boston, and shortly we were trimmed out at fifteen hundred feet. As we slid into the downwind leg, still at fifteen hundred feet, I wondered what Trig was planning to do, since it was obvious that we couldn't land on the airport from that altitude, especially from so close in, and I was more than a little surprised when he told me to ask the tower for permission to land. I looked sidewise at him with some doubt while I spoke to the tower, because we were so awfully high—as high as the Empire State Building—and the end of the runway was almost under my window. But, undaunted, Trig pulled on the carb heat, cut the throttle, held the nose up to kill the speed and hauled the flap handle between us all the way up, "click, click, click, click; then pointed her down like a Navy SBD in a thirty-five degree dive, right at the big white number painted on the end of the runway. He seemed to know what he was doing, but all I could do was sit there humming "The Wabash Cannon Ball" and hope for the best. About halfway down, the overhead speaker broke in excitedly, "Cessna two two Charlie discontinue and go around."

"Hell, he didn't think we could make it," muttered Trig to himself as much as to me.

"That's two of us," I answered darkly. He grinned, as he opened the throttle and climbed to two thousand feet.

"We'll fool him this time," he said, when we got back on base leg. "Ask him if we can make a 'touch and go' landing." I did so, and got an "affirmative," so Trig again pulled the flaps, shoved the wheel, and down we went. Despite our steep angle of descent, the airspeed hung right on eighty mph and by gum, it was clear that we were going to hit that "14" painted on the end of the runway. How hard I wasn't sure yet. As he came back a little on the wheel, Trig said to me, "Tell 'em we're going to complete," and, as I passed the word, I looked at the tower. There were three sets of saucer-sized eyes watching us, waiting for us to be mashed. Trig eased her back into a flare out, dumped the flaps so that we settled into the ground as if a magnet had been turned on, and slammed on the brakes. No one was more surprised than the boys in the tower, not even me. We didn't even get to the taxi strip on our roll out.

"Fun?" asked Trig, with an impish grin, which I couldn't help returning.

"I still don't trust that nose wheel," I answered, "it doesn't give the prop enough clearance from the ground." The next thing I knew we were taxiing in a zigzag course at a high rate of speed over the rough ground at the edge of the field, jolting and bouncing, but the prop never touched the ground and the plane handled beautifully, under all conditions of abuse.

Three more times I took off and landed the 172 and, with each flight, I was impressed still further with its sterling performance. I was aware of all the magnificent slow-flight characteristics that all the Cessnas have, but it seemed to me that there was nothing that could touch this one on ground stability and handling qualities, especially for short-field operations.

"How about sand?" I asked Trig.

"Cinch," he said, laconically.

"High grass?"

"Slows you up a little, but you sure won't nose over," he answered.

By this time I could feel that dull pounding sensation at the base of my skull, for this airplane was by far the safest, most practical airplane for week-end pilots that I had run into.

"How much?" I asked Trig, when we finally stepped out of the plane.

"About fifteen thousand dollars, with radio," he answered, patting the cowling. He might just as well have said, "Fifteen million," as far as I was concerned. I was going to have a struggle to buy a used plane, and here I was blithely inquiring about one fresh from the factory.

"Can I finance it?" I asked, as we strolled back to the *Legal Eagle*.

"Sure," he said, "sell this plane, use the dough as a down payment, and finance the rest."

"Sell this plane." It sounded so commercial. Sell your child. Sell your dog. Sell your plane.

I pulled the starter knob on the 140 as he slid into the right seat, and a few minutes later, he was crawling out at his own field and my son was getting in. As Trig stood protected from the slip stream by the half-opened door, we shook hands good-by, and he said to King, "Ask your Dad about the 172." Then he ducked back, waved, and we were off for Wings.

"What'zis about a 172?" asked King, kidlike, so I told him the story.

All the way back to Wings in my 140, we talked it over, and I was thinking. The young man had agreed to buy the *Eagle,* but, nevertheless, how could I afford to pay for the 172? I finally answered the question for myself: I couldn't. A 170 B, maybe. The 172, no. Tough.

Seven days usually seems like a long time, but that week passed with the speed of light; foreboding accelerated it, I guess, for my sentimental feelings for the *Eagle* made me want to hang on to her just as long as I could.

Paradoxically, it seems that one of the best, and at the same time, worst, traits of the human mind is the recurrent effect of this small spark called "sentiment" that from time to time rises into prominence in our mental processes and shoulders logic aside, just when it is most needed for making serious decisions. We men make fun of our womenfolks, saying patronizingly that they think with their hearts, not their heads. But let's admit it—

there are times when we all do, and I am not ashamed one bit that I have done so. The sale of my beloved little 140 had a depressing effect on me. Although some cynical people may doubt and deny that a Philadelphia lawyer could develop an emotional attachment to a machine, mine was great enough that I almost backed out of the deal.

Saturday dawned gray and sullen, although flyable. The weather reflected my mood perfectly as I arrived at Wings alone, for I didn't want anyone else around that day, not even my oldest son.

For the last time I took the ropes off zero four four and lovingly ran my hand over the cool metal of her sides, remembering the miles she had wafted me through the air. I checked her out, just as I had done so many times before: wrench the prop, shake the wing, kick the tires. Gee, I felt lousy. It was as if I were going to a funeral as we rolled down the runway and she sprang like a dove into the air.

That day, on the flight to Bethlehem, I felt the way I had when I cradled my dog, hit by a drunken driver, in my arms until he died. It didn't last too long. I couldn't even stay with her a little longer by getting lost, it seemed: I hit the airport right on the nose, landed and taxied up to the line, where Trig and his student stood waiting.

I eased out of the plane, we shook hands and went into the office. In five minutes it was all over. I signed the bill of sale and took a certified check in full payment.

As we went over to Trig's 170 for the ride back to Wings, I detoured a few feet to take one last look at the *Legal Eagle* standing there so pretty and lonely on the grass, knowing I would never fly her again.

"So long, pal," I said softly, then turned away and never looked back.

Another blow fell when I got back to Wings: The 170 B that I wanted had been sold to someone else while I was scratching for the money with which to buy it; so for the second time within a period of a few months I was without an airplane, and I felt terrible. In a sense my suffering was akin to what doctors call the "withdrawal symptoms" of the narcotic addict whose supply of dope has been cut off, for flying truly had a narcotic effect on me from the first. It generated a feeling of well-being, a certain ebullience; my troubles evaporated. I was happiest when flying, or thinking of flying. Narcotic addicts colloquially define their addiction by saying they are "hooked," that they "have a monkey on their back." From my reactions to being planeless, I realized that I was "hooked." You might say that I had a "Cessna on my back," so to speak.

Something had to happen and it did.

It was a bright Sunday morning. The air was as clear as a crystal and my wife and I were taking a drive on the way home from church, when I found myself on the expressway, headed for Wings. Feeling like a stranger as we pulled into the parking space, I heard Marianne say, "What's *that*?" And I saw that parked on the grass sat a Cessna 172.

"Do you like it?" I asked guardedly, as we walked over to it.

"Looks funny," she said, as a man came around the corner towards us, wearing a white campaign button on his lapel.

"May I help you?" he said, introducing himself as a Cessna dealer, just in on a delivery from the factory.

"I flew one of these a couple of weeks ago and wanted

my wife to see it," I said lamely, drooling at the pretty plane.

"Sit in here and see how you like it," said the affable pilot, addressing himself to my spouse—no fool, he. Never underestimate the power of a woman, and all that.

Marianne sat in the left front seat behind the controls.

"This is *roomy*," she said meaningfully to me, a reflection on the small cabin of the 140. "I love the upholstery; it seems like a car," she said. Then, "What's this thing—the hand brake?"

"That, my dear young lady, is the flap handle," answered the salesman, who picked up the ball faster than Phil Rizzuto.

"How about a ride?" he asked, sliding into the right seat. She looked at me with a funny expression, then the door slammed and I was cut off from their conversation. I could see Marianne pointing and asking questions and the salesman explaining things, then I heard her feminine voice call, "Clear," and the metal prop turned once, the engine growled power, and they started to roll.

As the 172 rocked over the grass to the end of the runway, I picked up a copy of the *New Yorker*, which I found lying on a bench in front of the office and leafed through it. On page 40, I saw the ubiquitous advertisement asking the question, "Who, *me* fly?" the new slogan of Cessna. I dropped the magazine to my lap as the 172 took off and circled the field, to land, take off, and land again; then it took off and disappeared to the east. I went into the coffee shop and drank a cup of java and, by the time I finished, saw the 172 rolling up to the line.

The big left door opened and my wife stepped out smiling. As she and the Cessna man approached I noticed that the white campaign button had been transferred from his lapel to hers and wondered what had been going on up there.

"I took off and landed it myself," chortled my wife, before I could ask my questions. "That's a terrific airplane, with room for all the family and easy to handle and . . ." As she came closer, I read the printing on the white button for the first time—the Cessna slogan, "Who, *me* fly?"

My mouth dropped open but, in a few seconds, I got it under control again, closed it, opened it and asked, "Who, *you* fly?"

A glint came into the soft brown eyes of the gal who used to hate flying, and who, for two years, had been cool to all suggestions that she take a trip by air. For fully five seconds she didn't say anything; then a smile spread across her face and she nodded slightly *"Me fly!"*

Never try to figure women because, no matter what a man thinks a woman is going to do, she will invariably cross him up. I have been married to the same lady for more than fifteen years, and foolishly believed that I could tell her every thought before she expressed it, merely because we had been, in law, "one person" for all that time; but I forgot the first important lesson I ever learned at my father's knee—that women's clutch of logic slips like crazy.

How a woman can, with perfect equanimity, not flicking an eyelash, change her mind completely, is a frightening sight to behold; a chameleon cannot change its color as fast as a woman can change her mind, and the chameleon has an advantage—its changes don't cost money.

Driving home I didn't say a word, trying to figure what her game was, for she kept chattering about how we could fly to Florida and Cuba and New Orleans and all sorts of places, with our kids, with our friends and by ourselves. Yakity-yak.

"Just what is she getting at?" I wondered, as a husband of long standing, lying and jumping through the hoop, as the occasion required, trying to analyze her approach. I finally got it; she was using "wife psychology" on me. Knowing that I would think of an argument against any position she would take, she was cannily suggesting that I buy a new airplane, to which I would react by making an argument against buying the plane; in other words, I would make her argument for her. Ho! Ho! I wasn't to be fooled by her; I wouldn't say a word. I didn't have a chance to. For two days she talked about nothing but the 172, until I finally told her to "lay off."

"What's the matter?" she asked, sitting on my lap, and trying to smooth the knots out of my forehead with a cool hand.

"You know what's the matter," I fumed, "I want that 172 like the dickens, but I can't afford to pay ten thousand dollars for a new plane and there aren't any used 172's yet. If I had a business in which I could use it, it would be easy, but I don't. It's just a sport with me, so let's forget it before I snap my cap!"

"Young man," she suddenly said, sternly seizing me by both shoulders and shaking me, "I've been married to you for fifteen years and I've never seen you want anything yet that you didn't get. I know you will find a way to get that 172, so we can all be week-end pilots, even if you have to start a new business.

Her remarks were so ridiculous that they broke the tension, and I threw back my head and laughed. "You nut," I answered, "you character! Start a new business?

I don't have the time! Where do you get these ideas? I could write a book!"

"Why don't you?" she said, snappily.

Something clicked. I reached for a yellow pad and wrote, "*Week-end Pilot* by Frank K. Smith."

"Don't stop with that," she said. "Go ahead—*write it!*"

I began to think back over the past two years, and of how I used to be a positive type of person. Dogmatic . . . I began to scribble. . . . .

And so I wrote this book.

15. My Head Is in the Clouds

Two years ago I was a sick cookie, overworked, over-wrought and overextended. I was always tired, always longing to lie down, yet, even after I fell into bed I couldn't sleep through the night, hence I was never rested. For me a week end was like the one-minute respite that a battered prize fighter works toward during the last rounds of a grueling battle; not really time enough to be rejuvenated, but only enough to enable him to take a deep breath and plunge back into the fray, hoping to last the distance.

By any comparison one can see that flying has had a tremendous effect on me, psychologically, philosophically and, indeed, physically. Today I have a spring in my step, a sparkle in my eye, a song in my heart and a feeling of readiness for come what may. The gnawing pain in my stomach—the hallmark of tension—has disappeared, and for the first time in years I can eat anything and I sleep like a baby. Flying has been my release, my catalyst, my outlet.

In recent years one of my most depressing concerns had been that I could never see the wonders of the United

States with my children; that we could not visit those places with the romantic names: Yosemite National Park, Mammoth Cave, the Grand Canyon, and that together we would never see San Francisco, New Orleans, Chicago, Boston, Salt Lake City. I have always wanted to go to Alaska, and to Texas; to look down on Las Vegas at night and Bar Harbor in the daytime. Two years ago long-range family travel was a mere dream, seemingly impossible of fulfillment, yet today it is almost a sure thing for as week-end pilots, in the 172 we can cross the entire country easily in two days.

For years I have been a conservationist and sportsman. My father taught me to love and to preserve God's great outdoors, with its lakes, streams and mountains teeming with wild life. I usually release the fish I catch and often go afield with a camera rather than a gun, but I like to sleep out under the stars, and I have the compelling yearning of a father to take my sons into the brush to learn to love nature just as my Dad did with me. The airplane is my pair of seven-league boots which will make all of these trips come true.

And nothing compares with the electric feeling of anticipation that fires my blood whenever I am at the controls of a light plane; the indescribable thrill of each take-off, the pure sensation of release, as the whirling propeller sucks me up into the airman's world.

I have great plans for the 172, plans that embrace Canada and Cuba and Central America, but I can't expect to fulfill them all at one time. I still have to earn a living, and I want to help young people who are not as fortunate as my children are, and I accept many more obligations than I should undertake, so my feet are still firmly planted on the ground. Sometimes it has seemed to me that I was chained to Philadelphia.

But, now when things get tense and problems seem insurmountable, I turn to the window, look up at the pale blue sky and see the fluffy clouds hanging there like so many puffs of angels' breath, and a voice says, "C'mon, Frank—c'mon up and play with us." Then I wink and say, "In a little while," and turn to solve the problems at hand with a placid mind, knowing that it won't be long until I am up there in my blue Heaven. I have finally achieved Nirvana. My feet may be on the ground, but my head is in the clouds.

FRANK KINGSTON SMITH was a successful Philadelphia lawyer following a harried business routine, when his doctor advised him to find a hobby. After trying everything from golf to model railroading, he discovered flying, and his life hasn't been the same since. Smith now lives in Washington, D.C., with his wife. He practices law and is a registered lobbyist representing aviation interests.

VINTAGE BIOGRAPHY AND AUTOBIOGRAPHY